"An incredibly timely book as many of us struggle to lead our children through the digital minefield of modern life. Richard Culatta avoids the pitfalls of preaching about the evils of technology, and instead guides us to a safe path of good, balanced behaviors that are applicable in all of our homes and schools."

—**LORD JIM KNIGHT,** Chair, Centre for the Acceleration of Social Technology; former Minister of State for Schools (UK)

"As a journalist and a parent, I appreciate the specific, positive, and actionable steps Culatta lays out for teaching our kids and ourselves how to be better digital citizens."

—**MANOUSH ZOMORODI,** host, *TED Radio Hour*; author, *Bored and Brilliant*

"Richard Culatta has written an engaging book, filled with personal stories as a parent and technologist. *Digital for Good* provides a fresh look at navigating the ever-evolving digital world with kids."

—**LINDA BURCH,** Chief Strategy Officer, Common Sense Media

DIGITAL for GOOD

DIGITAL for GOOD

RAISING KIDS to THRIVE in an ONLINE WORLD

RICHARD CULATTA

Harvard Business Review Press
Boston, Massachusetts

Library of Congress Cataloging-in-Publication Data

Names: Culatta, Richard E. (Richard Edward), 1978- author.
Title: Digital for good : raising kids to thrive in an online world / Richard Culatta.
Description: Boston, Massachusetts : Harvard Business Review Press, [2021] |
    Includes index.
Identifiers: LCCN 2021003226 (print) | LCCN 2021003227 (ebook) |
ISBN 9781647820169 (hardcover) | ISBN 9781647820176 (ebook)
Subjects: LCSH: Internet and youth. | Internet—Moral and ethical aspects.|
    Internet—Social aspects. | Technology and youth. | Technology—Moral and
    ethical aspects. | Technology—Social aspects.
Classification: LCC HQ799.9.I58 C78 2021 (print) | LCC HQ799.9.I58
    (ebook) | DDC 004.67/8083—dc23
LC record available at https://lccn.loc.gov/2021003226
LC ebook record available at https://lccn.loc.gov/2021003227

ISBN: 978-1-64782-016-9
eISBN: 978-1-64782-017-6

To Anna, James, Benjamin, and Eli.
Our digital future is bright in your hands.
Also, go clean your rooms.

CONTENTS

DIGITAL for GOOD

INTRODUCTION

Welcome Home(s)

Congratulations! You are among the first humans tasked with simultaneously raising kids in both physical and digital worlds. The physical world is, of course, where we all live. It's the playground we take our kids to, the bus where we sit next to people on the way to work, and the neighborhoods where we ride our bikes. It's the world our parents raised us in.

But our kids are also growing up in a digital world—a parallel universe we access through computers, tablets, smartphones, and wearable devices. It's where we go to get our news, order groceries, and meet with our teams as we work remotely.

We have a dual citizenship that allows us to move seamlessly between these two worlds hundreds of times a day without even realizing it. Our kids have no memory of a time when they didn't have access to both worlds. It has never crossed their minds that there was once a time when you couldn't buy a skateboard on Amazon or stream episodes of *The Mandalorian* on a smartphone. Yet, as familiar as the digital world has become, we have put surprisingly little effort into making sure our kids are prepared to be safe and healthy when they're there. We provide our children with all kinds of preparation to be successful in the physical world. We schedule regular health checkups and encourage them to put on sunscreen and wear helmets. We teach them to play nicely with the other kids at the playground, to ask permission before going to someone else's house, and say "thank you" when they leave. We teach them to hold the door open for someone carrying bags of groceries, to be considerate of others, and much, much more.

But when it comes to preparing our kids to be successful in the digital world, it's like the proverbial crickets. With viral misinformation campaigns, cyberbullying, and exploitation of our personal data, we simply cannot afford to be haphazard in this responsibility. Fortunately, we can close this gap and proactively prepare our children to thrive in digital spaces by understanding more about how the virtual world works and applying some surprisingly simple strategies for teaching our kids to use technology as a force for good in their lives.

We Are All Connected

Our digital universe has put us in contact with exponentially more people than someone who grew up in the physical world only. I often think about the difference between the life of my grandfather and that of my son. In 1929, when Salvatore Culatta was just fourteen years old, he boarded the *SS Providence* and traveled from Palermo, Italy, to New York City. At that time, the number of people he could have interacted with was largely a calculation of how many people lived within a fifty-mile physical radius of wherever he was and how much time he could devote to going new places. Even as phones became more widespread, the telephone generally connected people who already knew each other, so the circle of people my grandpa would have interacted with wouldn't have grown exponentially throughout his lifetime.

That is not the case for my son, Benjamin Sal (who is named after his great-grandpa), thanks to a little Department of Defense project known as ARPANET. This computer-to-computer network became the backbone of today's internet in the nineties when Tim Berners-Lee figured out how to use the network to create the World Wide Web. Anyone with a computer and a web browser could now view "pages" stored on internet web servers. The rest, as they say, is history. But today's internet is about much more than just connecting computers and viewing web pages. This worldwide network is about connecting people to each other without the barriers of time, travel, language, or any of the other constraints that limit people from interacting with each other in the physical world.

At any given point in our day, through the digital world, we are all just a few degrees of separation from anyone else on the planet. Through the internet, my son has the potential to be in contact with as many people in a day as his grandfather had in a year—or some people have had in their entire lifetimes. This exponential access to other people fundamentally shifts the realities and possibilities of the world our children are growing up in. The artificial barrier of physical location will never be a constraint that limits access to who they work with, play with, and learn from.

The Digital Migration

The digital world is also quickly replacing the physical world as the host site for many of our most important daily activities. As the world grappled with the reality of the Covid-19 pandemic, it also led us to reset our expectations for what types of activities we could do as (or more) successfully in online spaces. We have now become a digital workforce, with the majority of professionals reporting to work in the virtual world.[1] Medical advice has migrated from doctors' offices to sites like Healthline.com, and appointments with specialists are conducted virtually through a variety of telehealth apps.[2]

When we're in the mood to see a movie or watch our favorite TV show, 75 percent of US households turn to Netflix or other streaming media services for entertainment. By putting on an Oculus headset, we can turn our living rooms into an African safari or the international space station. Thanks to Amazon and its competitors, over 90 percent of the US population is expected to shop online, as everything from prescription glasses to diapers are delivered conveniently to our door by mail and soon by drone.[3] Statistically speaking, it's also much less likely that we will meet our significant other in the physical world, as finding a date has almost entirely migrated to the digital world as well.[4] If OkCupid's twelve sexual orientation categories aren't specialized enough for us, custom dating sites let us find a farmer (FarmersOnly.com), a sea captain (SeaCaptainDate.com), or even a double date for us and our pet (DateMyPet.com).[5]

When Covid-19 hit and 1.2 billion students worldwide left brick-and-mortar classrooms, school migrated to the virtual world. Even before Covid-19, the number of college students taking only online courses in the United States was growing by more than 350,000 a year.[6] BYJU'S (India's top online learning site) teaches 35 million students a year, and VIPKid employs over 65,000 US teachers to deliver 180,000 English classes virtually to students in China every day. Informal learning has almost entirely migrated to the digital world as well (86 percent of YouTube viewers say they go there to learn something new).[7]

Some less obvious but equally transformational migrations to the digital world have also taken place. Ghost kitchens—restaurants with, well, no restaurant—have begun to emerge.[8] People place their virtual orders directly with the chefs who prepare the food and then communicate (also virtually) with delivery services like DoorDash that deliver the food to their doorstep. We pay for our meals using virtual banks that, like the ghost kitchens, don't have any physical presence. In some countries, all financial transactions have already moved entirely to the virtual world, making paper money obsolete. On a recent trip to China, I couldn't find a single store that would accept a credit card, much less paper money. Retail financial transactions in China take place by scanning a QR code into WeChat (China's version of Face-book). Homeless people on the streets had QR codes on cardboard signs asking for digital handouts. Around the world, registering to vote—and even voting itself—is shifting into the virtual world.[9]

Digital migration has been accelerated by unfathomable increases in computing power. The phone in my pocket has 120 million times the processing power of the computers that took the first astronauts to the moon![10] With new networks on the horizon promising increased bandwidth and zero latency (that annoying delay you experience when talking to someone on a video chat), a whole host of additional activities will soon migrate to the virtual world. We will soon be able to go to a local orchestra concert where the guest conductor is join-ing by holograph from anywhere in the world. Today, to undergo an appendectomy, you must be physically in the same room as the doc-tor, which limits the availability of lifesaving medical attention. With next-generation wireless networks, telesurgery will enable doctors to operate remotely from anywhere in the world. Technology brings an unprecedented level of convenience and personalization, and it will allow our children to do more, learn more, create more, and connect more than any of us could have ever imagined.

The migration from the physical to the digital world represents a fundamental shift in the lives of our children. The events that take place in the virtual world are not ancillary to their lives but are some of the most important elements of them. The limitations of the phys-ical world will not shape or constrain the design of our children's life events the way they did mine or yours.

Houston, We Have a Problem

Despite the limitless possibilities, there is a dark side to the digital world my son—and all of our children—has access to. For all the good the virtual world has to offer, it is also filled with some wicked problems.

Most of them stem from one fundamental flaw: we never took the time to establish the ground rules for meaningful participation. We have spent the last two decades excitedly finding ways to migrate all kinds of experiences to the digital world, but we haven't stopped to ask how we will preserve our civil society as it also migrates there. With no expectation for acceptable behavior and near-complete anonymity, we have created an environment that is optimized for self-destruction.

We need to commit to establishing expectations for meaningful and civil online behaviors that will allow our children to not only be their best selves online, but bring out the best in others as well. I refer to the attributes and norms for responsible and healthy behavior in virtual spaces as *digital citizenship*. Effective digital citizens are those who know how to engage respectfully with other members of the virtual world and use technology to improve their digital and physical communities. If we can't figure out how to create a generation of positive, productive, and civil online inhabitants, our amazing parallel universe will eventually turn into one in which none of us will want to live—and it will be too late to migrate back. The consequences of getting it wrong are disastrous and irrecoverable. The goal of this book is to start a new conversation to help our kids thrive in virtual spaces—to teach them to become contributing digital citizens who can positively shape the virtual world and the activities within it. This book is the user's guide for the digital world that we never created.

We'll begin in chapter 1 by identifying four digital dysfunctions that affect how we operate in digital spaces, exploring the risks of not addressing these key problems. Chapter 2 then looks at the issues with our current way of teaching online expectations to children, both what we've gotten wrong so far and what we can do about it. It makes the urgent case that teaching online safety isn't enough; we need a more comprehensive approach to creating future digital citizens. Chapters 3 through 7 then break down that approach by discussing five practical digital citizenship skills that all kids need to learn: being balanced, informed, inclusive, engaged, and alert. Finally, in the remaining two chapters, we will meet the other members of our team and what we can expect the digital world to look like in the future.

As I point out some of the dysfunction that exists in our virtual world, I wouldn't blame you if your gut reaction is to bury all of your family's mobile devices in the backyard. There are certainly others who suggest taking that route. I recently learned about a movement that encourages parents to pledge to keep their children off any devices until eighth grade. Some claim to have heard that Silicon Valley tech CEOs won't let their own kids use technology (as far as I can tell, that idea comes from a misinterpreted interview with Steve Jobs from a decade ago).[11]

Yes, digging the hole in the backyard might make us feel better in the short term, but it also takes away the opportunity for our children to learn good habits at a young age. It's a bit like saying we should not teach our kids to read in order to keep them from being exposed to hate speech. Cutting children off from devices entirely can actually increase the risks and dangers, as they lose important opportunities to develop healthy digital habits. To become lifelong learners, provide for their families, and become leaders of our civil society, our children must learn how to responsibly use digital tools from a young age. The problem isn't the technology; it's that we haven't established the right expectations for participation in the digital world. Establishing expectations for our kids and holding tech platforms accountable for creating healthy online communities is harder than digging that hole. But it is one of the most important things we can do as parents to ensure a healthy and happy future.

Meet Your Tour Guide

My journey with technology started as a nerdy kindergartner when my mom decided we should get an Apple IIe computer so I could learn the skills of the future. Because of her job at the University of Rhode Island, I also got access to Gopher and Telnet—early versions of the internet—which opened my mind to the possibility of connecting with experts anywhere in the world at the click of a button. Fast-forward a bit and I found myself working in the US Senate, where I saw how that same technology I played with as a kid could bring the voices of constituents right into our offices in Washington, DC. Years later, as the chief innovation officer for my home state, I again turned to technology to make college more accessible, our cities safer, and to transform our students into problem-solvers, by becoming the first state to teach computer science in every school.

In 2012, President Obama appointed me to lead the Office of Educational Technology for the US Department of Education. While serving in the Obama administration, I saw firsthand how tech could make it easier for first-generation college students to plan and apply for college, increase veterans' access to medical benefits, and identify potential terrorists before they could harm our country. My role gave me the opportunity to work closely with the world's largest tech companies. I've had a unique behind-the-scenes view of technical capabilities that make me proud to be human. In my current role as the CEO of the International Society for Technology in Education (ISTE), a nonprofit serving educators in a hundred countries, my work is focused on using technology to make sure all students have access to high-quality learning opportunities adapted to meet their individual needs.

My wife, Shaundra, and I have four wonderful children, and we are fortunate to rely on lessons we learned from our own parents as we try to teach teach our kids to make good decisions, be respectful to others, and follow good examples. Despite having spent my career at the intersection of tech and learning, we realized how entirely unprepared we were to help our own children develop the skills they needed to thrive in the virtual world. When it came time for the "birds and the bees" talk, we laughed at the memory of the awkward moment when our parents tried to explain where babies come from, but even that cringey memory provided a baseline for us to improve on and adapt as we try to teach our kids the same thing.

Parents and teachers don't have any baseline for preparing our kids to be effective digital citizens. Many books and blogs seem more focused on shocking us with the dangers of technology than providing strategies for how to teach our kids to use tech to enrich their lives. Books like *The Boogeyman Exists: And He's in Your Child's Back Pocket* or *The Dumbest Generation: How the Digital Age Stupefies Young Americans and Jeopardizes Our Future* frighten us and ignore the consequences of not teaching our kids to use tech for good. None of the evidence that we observed in raising our own kids, or that I've seen as I've worked with education systems worldwide, would suggest that technology is making our kids dumber; in fact, I've found exactly the opposite to be true.

As I've talked to parents, I quickly discovered my wife and I aren't alone. This fueled my journey to find strategies that can help parents and teachers set up their kids for success. This book is for parents, community leaders, and educators who can use some thoughtful insights on how to raise amazing kids in the evolving digital world. There may be moments as you are reading that the thought may pop into your mind, "I wish I had known these ideas earlier. Now that my kids are older, is it too late to start?" Let me state now that it is never too late to change a family's digital culture. Of course, certain principles are easier to put in place before a child has spent much time in the digital world or before they receive their first smartphone. But even if your children have been online for some time, it is not too late to rethink the way you are preparing them to thrive in the virtual world. Whether you're a parent or teacher to toddlers, tweens, teenagers, or some age in between, you can apply the tools in this book to shape your children into healthy digital citizens—and even learn to apply them to improve your own digital habits.

When thinking about adapting and changing a school's or family's digital culture, it is important to do it *with* your kids and not *to* them; involve older kids, who will have suggestions based on habits developed from their own digital experiences. Talk about *why* it is important to practice being an effective digital citizen. Help them see the difference they can make in their life and the lives of others based on their behaviors in the virtual world. Identify the good and bad elements of your existing family culture when it comes to using technology (what do you do well as a family; where are you weaker?). Identify concerns that they may have about making changes (e.g., how will I wake up on time if my phone isn't next to my bed?). Changing culture doesn't happen in a single talk, but in an ongoing conversation. And remember that just because you are getting input from your kids, there can still be elements of your family culture that you determine as nonnegotiable as well.

My goal is for us to start a new conversation about raising kids in a digital world, one that we should have been having for a long time. Not a conversation based on fear or avoiding technology, but on applying the good parenting and teaching skills we're already familiar with from the physical world to ensure success for our kids in the virtual world. If we do it right, we will create a better future for them and us, and we'll look back on our efforts with pride and toward the future with hope.

1

Our Digital Dysfunction

've always been fascinated with airplanes. As a kid, I had posters of planes on the walls of my room. In college, I worked as a crew member for an experimental-aircraft festival. As a young father, I took my kids to the airport to play "airplane bingo," where we'd try to figure out what type of plane was taking off before it passed overhead. When my wife needed a quiet house on Saturdays to give violin lessons, I took the kids to hang out in the National Air and Space Museum.

About ten years ago, with a nudge from my daughter, I decided to learn how to fly a plane myself. Like all new pilots, I started by earning a private pilot's license that allowed me to fly a plane in visual conditions. Just like driving a car, when flying in visual conditions, you make all flying decisions by looking out the window, seeing where you're going, and adjusting based on what you see. If it looks as if you're headed toward another plane, you turn in a different direction. To make sure you're flying level, you look at where the horizon lines up against the nose of the plane and adjust your wings until they are parallel. When landing, you look for the runway and adjust your speed and altitude to land. We could get away with only having visual pilots except for one thing: clouds. When you're in the clouds, you can't see anything. Even though the fundamental approach for flying the plane is the same, your reference point for making all of your decisions (what you can see out the window) is now gone.

Instrument flying teaches pilots to use the equipment in the plane to avoid crashing into other airplanes, keep flying level, and land safely even when they can't see anything outside the window. When I began working on getting my instrument license, I found one of the hardest parts was learning to trust the instruments over my gut feelings. When you can't see the visual cues you're accustomed to, your gut sends you all kinds of incorrect messages. Every year, visual pilots inadvertently end up flying into the clouds. Even though the physics of flying the plane haven't changed, they haven't learned how to use the instruments as their primary reference point. Most visual pilots who accidentally get into the clouds end up completely upside down in less than three minutes because they don't know how to recognize and correct their own behavior.[1]

Our access to the digital world has dramatically changed the way we navigate through life. And because these changes came without precedent or instruction, we have almost entirely relied on our natural inclinations—what worked in the physical world—to determine how to behave in this new space. Just as in flying a plane, even though the fundamentals of being an effective member of a human community haven't changed, when we are in an unfamiliar environment and we don't understand how to use the tools that will keep us flying level, our gut inclinations don't always serve us well. According to Renee Hobbs, professor of media literacy at the University of Rhode Island, two-thirds of American families don't have any strategy for using digital media in their homes. As a society, we are visual pilots who have found ourselves in a digital cloud without the training we need to be there. Indicators of our digital dysfunction are everywhere. We're in the clouds and upside down.

Before we can talk about the strategies to safely navigate our digital world, we need to first understand some of the dangers that exist around us. We'll start by looking at four representative examples of our digital dysfunction that threaten the success of our children and the future of our civil society. As I stated in the introduction, this is not a gloom and doom book. But being optimistic about our digital future doesn't mean ignoring the dangers. My goal isn't to make an exhaustive list of all the problems in our digital world but instead to provide a few reference points to underscore the urgency of getting things right.

A Dystopia for Clicking Ads

The first digital dysfunction stems from the underlying business model of the internet. Our online platforms are largely financed by advertisements. This leads us to ruthlessly bombard our children with upwards of three thousand ads per day.[2] Research from the American Psychological Association shows that children younger than eight are cognitively and psychologically defenseless against advertising. They don't understand the concept of "selling" and therefore accept advertising claims at face value. And remember, these are not old school newspaper ads or the commercials for Crystal Pepsi that appeared between episodes of *The Simpsons* while we were growing up. The online ads we are feeding to our children are blended with nonadvertising content in a way that makes them much harder to distinguish. Most children can't even tell which part of a website is an advertisement and which isn't.[3] The user experience of the web itself has evolved to spread the information we're looking for across multiple pages in order to create more traps for targeted ads.

Digital ads are highly optimized to take advantage of our unique weaknesses. Using our own viewing and purchasing history, collected by companies like Acxiom and LiveRamp, complex algorithms learn our specific behavioral patterns. They then use that data to make highly accurate predictions about our future behaviors and modify advertising to be optimally irresistible at just the right moment. This is known as persuasion architecture. How well does it work? A couple of years ago the *New York Times* broke the story of a father who demanded an apology from Target for sending his teenage daughter ads for baby clothes and diapers. While he didn't know it yet, Target's algorithms had already figured out that his daughter was pregnant based on her digital footprint. Target can not only tell which of its customers are pregnant but estimate the due date within a surprisingly accurate window based only on their online behavior.[4]

The constant diet of virtual advertising is causing some very real problems. For starters, parent-child conflicts increase as parents deny purchase requests that were precipitated by advertising. Then there's the worrisome connection between viewing targeted advertising and decisions young people make. Carefully targeted e-cigarette ads have correlated with millions of middle and high school students who are now vaping.[5] Targeted advertising has had an impact on childhood obesity, as millions of kids choose to eat unhealthy foods when their favorite cartoon characters show up on the advertising.[6] Somehow Disney characters never seem to appear on packaging for broccoli. And because the rules that limit certain types of advertising on kids' TV programming don't yet apply on the internet, even carefully selected online videos or appropriate websites can be hijacked by disturbing advertising messages over which we have no control.

But the truly disconcerting part of our targeted-ad-driven internet is that we are permitting marketers to use our children's most intimate personal information to make them more easily deceived. Without realizing it, you are allowing your children's states of anxiety or depression, physical health, even the timing of your daughter's menstrual cycle, to be used for manipulating her behavior into making money for someone else.[7] And as a society, we are doing almost nothing to stop it. As sociologist Zeynep Tufekci explains in her eye-opening TED Talk, "We're building a dystopia just to make people click on ads."[8] If someone who wasn't already accustomed to our digital dysfunction were to observe this behavior, they would easily conclude that we are systematically exploiting our children as part of an income-generation scheme for someone we don't even know.

Digital Exploitation and Abuse

Another digital dysfunction is the deliberate interpersonal harm that increasingly taints our virtual world. Taking the form of bullying, hate speech, and exploitation, this shocking cruelty festers in innumerable cases around the digital world. Amanda Todd was a typical Canadian teenager. She loved singing, art, animals, and snowflakes. Her favorite color was purple.[9] Amanda moved to a new school in seventh grade and used video chats to meet new people. She would sing and dance on camera, and generally enjoyed the attention and compliments she received. People told her she was "beautiful, stunning, perfect." During one chat, though, someone convinced her to flash her breasts.[10] Soon after, Amanda, then only thirteen, got a message on Facebook from a stranger who threatened that if she didn't show more of herself, he would publish the topless pictures of her. The images were posted to a porn site and a link was sent to her Facebook friends. Amanda began experiencing anxiety, depression, and panic disorder.

In an attempt to escape, her family decided to move to a new home, to start fresh. A year later, her blackmailer reappeared. He created a Facebook profile that used Amanda's topless photo as the profile image and began contacting classmates at her new school. Amanda said, "[I] cried every night, lost all my friends and respect people had for me . . . again." She moved once more, to another city, another school, but the messages and abuses continued. The following September, Amanda posted a YouTube video called "My Story: Struggling, bullying, suicide, self harm."[11] Using a series of flashcards, she tells this painful story from her point of view. "I've decided to tell you about my never ending story," the first card in Amanda's hands reads. Shortly after posting her video on YouTube, Amanda hanged herself in her home.

Cyberbullying is any abuse or harassment that takes place in the digital world through text messaging, social media, even multiplayer gaming, where an unlimited and uncontrolled audience can view and share content. Cyberbullying can take many forms, including sharing negative, harmful, or threatening content about someone else. It often includes sharing personal or private information about an individual in an attempt to cause embarrassment or humiliation. There are several aspects of cyberbullying that make it significantly more problematic than bullying in the physical world. The first is scale. As strange as it may sound, in the physical world, it takes *effort* to bully someone (you have to physically track them down to interact with them), which can actually help limit the scale of damage. However, in the virtual world, a harmful comment or demoralizing picture can instantly be shared widely with peers and strangers with as little effort as a click or tap.

Not only is bullying easier online, but the perpetrator is also more removed from the consequences. The virtual world allows us to do and say things we would never attempt in person, simply because the distance shields us from experiencing the real-time, in-person results of our actions. We don't see the hurt in the other person's face or the disapproval of onlookers, or receive correction from authority— all factors that deter cruel behaviors in our physical spaces. And because we haven't done nearly enough to teach our children that the consequences of digital behaviors are just as—and sometimes much more—serious than the ones that come from physical behaviors, we are not making much progress in improving the problem.

While bullying in the physical world is generally limited to specific locations (for example, at the bus stop, in the locker room, and so on), cyberbullying is relentless. This means that the safe spaces a child can retreat to and not experience physical bullying, like their home, a church youth group, or a friend's house, are unavailable to escape cyberbullying. When the bullying takes place through a mobile device, there is literally no moment during the day or night when the person can get away from their attackers. Amanda's case is not unique in the sense that even moving to new schools or states does not ensure the bullying will stop. Proximity doesn't matter in digital spaces. The anonymity of the internet can make it very difficult to tell who the perpetrator is, which in turn makes it ever harder to stop. We have become entirely complacent with a digital culture that permits virtual bullying and abuse with little or no consequences. A recent Pew Research Center study showed that nearly 60 percent of US teens have been bullied or harassed online.[12] Even more shocking is the fact that almost 90 percent of teens have witnessed online bullying and most have done nothing about it.[13]

Our cyberbullying culture can't be blamed entirely on young people either. More than half of Americans have experienced hate speech and harassment online.[14] We see cyberbullying in the comments section of just about every news website. The *Guardian*'s analysis of nearly 1.5 million abusive comments from its site showed that articles written by women and nonwhite males consistently attracted a higher proportion of abusive comments.[15] Even global leaders—those we expect our children to see as role models and emulate—are complicit. Tweets from political leaders include name-calling, spreading rumors, and belittling nonpolitical aspects of their opponents. Sherri Gordon, a bullying prevention expert, says, "Children are observing the nation's top political leaders engaging in the very bullying tactics that kids at school use to climb the social ladder."[16]

Skewing Our Perception of Reality

A third dysfunction of our digital world is an increased tolerance for deception. Using digital tools, we've created a set of unrealistic baselines that skew our sense of reality and damage our self-perceptions. The digital world gives a platform from which we see into the intimate parts of other people's lives. As this happens, we can't help but compare their experiences to our own.

Comparison is a natural human tendency that can motivate us to improve our lives and work harder. But the digital world takes advantage of our brain's logic with an underhanded trick. Because we can choose how we want to portray ourselves in the virtual world, we often put a more positive or impressive version of ourselves on display. We don't post every problem or stress point we're dealing with; rather we focus on our achievements, opportunities, and exciting moments. As we scroll through our social feeds, though, we often forget this fact as we compare everyone else's picture-perfect fantasy lives with the reality of flaws and sadness in our own. University of Houston psychologist Mai-Ly Nguyen Steers calls this viewing "everyone else's highlights reel."[17] The *New York Times* reports that Americans spend about six times the amount of time washing dishes as playing golf, yet there are twice as many tweets reporting golfing than doing dishes. The Las Vegas budget hotel Circus and the luxurious hotel Bellagio each accommodate about the same number of people, but the Bellagio gets about three times as many check-ins on Facebook. Owners of luxury cars like BMWs and Mercedes are more than twice as likely to mention their cars on Facebook as owners of ordinary makes and models.[18] You get the point.

This comparison with a skewed baseline has led to increasing feelings of hopelessness and depression, particularly for young girls.[19] Brian Primack, the dean of the College of Education and Health Professions at the University of Arkansas, found that people who checked social media the most frequently had almost three times the risk of depression, compared with people who checked less often.[20] The UK's Royal Society for Public Health found that social media use in teens is linked with increased body-image issues in young people, who are the heaviest users of social media.[21] Apps like Facetune only fuel this problem by encouraging teens to filter any picture to make their lips look bigger and stomach look smaller before posting to social media.

The digital world is also skewing the reality of our sexual culture. Nearly three hours of new porn videos are uploaded to Pornhub every minute of every day. Pornhub's website alone reports 115 million visits per day.[22] That's the equivalent of the entire populations of Canada, Australia, Poland, and the Netherlands all visiting the site, which is just a fraction of the total overall daily porn traffic. In the same way our edited social media posts promote an idealized view of our lives, the porn industry uses digital media tools to promote an unrealistic version of sexuality that is increasingly focused on portraying violent acts and sexual abuse. This unrealistic baseline actually leads to real-world problems as it drives an increasingly violent sexual culture and skews our ability to have healthy relationships. Through porn, boys learn that aggressive sexual behavior is acceptable, and girls learn that such behavior is expected.[23]

False baselines have become a common part of our digital world. We've created a virtual space where you have to be an exceptional person to even tell the truth about who you really are. The problem with becoming an age of pretenders is that there always comes a day of reckoning. No one's body will ever look like it does after Facetune, no life is all roses and European vacations, and violent sexual acts hurt in real life and damage our ability to have fulfilling, healthy relationships. We have become a society of pretenders fueled by a digital artificial baseline.

Eroding Civility

A final category of digital dysfunction are activities that directly threaten our civil society. These include the increasing use of digital tools to spread misinformation and interfere with democratic processes. Our children are growing up in a world where cyberattacks will cause far more damage to their safety than a physical war or terrorist attack.

Our acceptance of the rampant creation and spread of false information in the digital world has highlighted our inability to distinguish fact from fiction online. The ability to make informed choices, a pillar of any functioning democracy, requires us to have access to reliable information. Until now, maintaining this fundamental pillar largely meant ensuring the press had the freedom to write about news without fear of retaliation. However, as social media becomes our primary source of information, our ability to make effective decisions is at risk in a way that never could have been imagined by our nation's founders. News is algorithmically prioritized by popularity, not credibility, making it harder by the day to tell truth from fiction online.

Among the most shared US news from 2017 was a story saying that NPR reported over 25 million Hillary Clinton votes as fraudulent, a story about a death row inmate eating a Bible for his last meal, and a story about a California school where children were forced to learn sharia law in class.[24] Despite being widely shared, all these stories were completely false. Panic escalated during the 2020 coronavirus pandemic when a decade-old map of global airline routes was relabeled as a map of the spread of Covid-19 infections. It was shared tens of millions of times and even picked up and broadcast by TV news outlets.[25] Twitter alone shares about 4 million tweets of blatantly fake news each month.[26]

While there is widespread agreement that misinformation is a problem in our virtual world, we seem to shrug it off, telling ourselves that it's more annoying than dangerous.[27] Or perhaps that the source is a well-intentioned but eccentric user of our media platforms. In so doing, we ignore the reality that viral misinformation is a military-grade weapon for weakening national security. If you need convincing, look no further than the amount of energy countries put into foreign misinformation efforts each year. Russia has mounted sophisticated and effective hacking campaigns against the United States aimed at causing national instability. The work is engineered by the Internet Research Agency (IRA), a Russian organization aimed at interfering with the US political system.[28] According to the *Atlantic*, the IRA's work is based on the philosophy that you could "tip the world toward revolution through psychological warfare and deception, exploiting the divisions and weaknesses of bourgeois society."[29] Using hacked emails and Facebook data, posts on a variety of divisive issues like gay rights, gun control, and immigration are used to cause chaos in our civil society and pit Americans against each other.[30] A report from Oxford University estimates that between 2015 and 2018, over 30 million users shared the IRA's Facebook and Instagram posts with their friends and family, liking, reacting to, and commenting on them along the way.[31] Veteran *Washington Post* journalist David Von Drehle reports, "Seizing opportunities on the lawless frontiers of social media, [Vladimir Putin] has stoked division, spread disinformation, fanned conspiracy theories and generally mind-gamed the American system."[32] Our susceptibility to exaggeratedly divisive social media makes us vulnerable to foreign destabilization campaigns without them ever having to set foot on US soil.

Our digital dysfunction has also weakened another critical pillar of a functioning democracy: free and fair elections. In 2018, we learned that our personal data was being used to manipulate election results on a global scale. The now infamous Cambridge Analytica was a company that used a survey app to gain access to data on 230 million Facebook users. Due to the lack of protections from Facebook on data sharing at the time, Cambridge Analytica was able to access personal information about not only all the people using its app but also all of their friends and friends' friends. Cambridge Analytica publicly bragged that it had amassed five thousand data points on almost every person in the United States. Using this massive data set, Cambridge Analytica then identified potential "persuadables"— people who were on the fence about a given political issue. The persuadables were the relatively small number of people whose opinion, if changed, would sway the result of an election. Cambridge Analytica's business model was to sell its "swaying" services to the highest bidder. If you could afford to pay $1 million a day, it would deliver the fence-sitters to you on a silver platter by bombarding them with targeted, shockingly manipulative, digital messages. Using the five thousand data points, it could craft posts in a highly personal way to guarantee an emotional reaction, thereby pushing just enough persuadables to change their views and shift an election. And it worked. Evidence suggests that Cambridge Analytica changed the results of elections in Australia, India, Kenya, Malta, Mexico, the United Kingdom, and the United States by manipulating voters based on their own stolen data.

More recently, the world witnessed the impacts of viral misinformation in January 2021 when the United States capitol was overtaken by a violent mob. The last time the US Capitol was overthrown was during the War of 1812 and never by Americans. In addition to the desecration of a historic building and multiple deaths, a free and fair election was called into question, deteriorating trust in the election process itself, all of which was the result of intentional misinformation shared online. Donald Trump used Twitter to disseminate baseless claims that the election was "stolen," fueling the violent storming of the Capitol. Digital misinformation fuels polarization as it allows anyone with any belief to feel artificially right and removes the burden of trying to reconcile our differences. According to social psychologist Jonathan Haidt, "Online political discussions (often among anonymous strangers) are experienced as angrier and less civil than those in real life; networks of partisans co-create worldviews that can become more and more extreme; disinformation campaigns flourish; violent ideologies lure recruits." Haidt goes on to say, "Citizens are now more connected to one another, on platforms that have been designed to make outrage contagious."[33]

A direct line connects our problem with viral misinformation to the weakening of our society. Reporter Von Drehle reminds us that when it comes to attacks on democracy, "the battlefield of choice is the internet." The most destructive attacks against our civil society today come from bytes, not bombs.

Technology Is (Just) an Accelerator

So we have some problems, serious ones. These examples of digital dysfunction give a glimpse into behaviors that put our health, happiness, and civility at risk. Like the visual pilot losing control over the plane when flying into the clouds, our digital dysfunction has exposed how little preparation we have received for controlling the use of technology in our lives, not to mention teaching our children how to do it.

To get back to flying level (to put it positively) or keep from crashing the human race into the ground, we have to understand how we got into the digital clouds in the first place. Finding the answer to that question could seem overwhelming. We could spend a decade conducting an anthropological study of the role of disintegrating societal values juxtaposed with an unfiltered capitalistic system driving our modern technology use. But before we commission that study, I believe there is actually a much simpler answer. Our digital dysfunction stems from the fact that we've forgotten that technology does not have a conscience. As silly as that may sound, it can be surprisingly easy to do. After all, we reveal our most intimate questions and concerns to Google, which responds to us with superhuman capacity and accuracy.

New York University professor Scott Galloway makes the compelling case that the only other entity that comes as close as Google to be trusted with our most intimate questions is God.[34] Meanwhile Facebook knows more about our family's and friends' interests than we do. When Facebook reminds us of a birthday we would have otherwise forgotten, it can feel as if Facebook actually *cares* about them. When we look at it that way, we can easily forget that the platforms we trust with our most intimate personal details don't actually care about us at all—or even recognize the value of the interactions they enable.

Technology is just an accelerator and, as such, will accelerate whatever tasks we apply it to. The same real-time video technology that can connect a grandma from one side of the country with her grandkids on the other can also enable a multibillion-dollar revenge-porn industry. The same open networks that enable unrestricted access to all the books and art of the world also enable phishing scams that steal $600 billion annually.[35] Technology can accelerate the spread of information but is absolutely ambivalent to whether the information it spreads is true. Technology can facilitate interactions between millions of people but is indifferent to whether their intentions are good.

Instead of thinking of technology as a trusted friend with a conscience, we might be better served by thinking of technology as a curved mirror. It magnifies who we are as people—both the good and the bad. It reflects the values of its users, but to an extreme. As artist and author James Bridle puts it, technology has the capacity to instantiate all of our most extraordinary, often hidden, desires and biases by encoding them into our digital world.[36] Humans have the responsibility to bring a conscience to virtual spaces, and we must actively teach the future inhabitants of our digital world how to do that. If we don't take action, our digital interactions will continue to devolve until civility has crumbled, kindness has eroded, and digital dysfunctions become the defining characteristics of our virtual personas.

But that future is also entirely avoidable. In addition to magnifying our desires and biases, technology also makes them visible in a way that allows us to change them. It's harder to pretend that our beliefs and desires don't exist when our news feeds are optimized around them in a very observable way. We have the option to focus technology's accelerating forces on improving our world and deepening our humanity. We can create a generation that grows up learning how to aim that curved mirror toward accelerating meaningful interactions and tackling tough problems in their communities. The conscience of our technology, it turns out, must be us.

2

The Urgent Need for Digital Citizenship

For as long as humans have existed, we have been part of communities. We are evolutionarily wired to collaborate around common interests that have kept us safe, happy, and alive for hundreds of thousands of years. Communities allow us to tackle challenges that are too complex for any one of us to address alone, from providing public safety and equitable public education to stopping environmental degradation or eradicating a disease through medical advances. Communities form around shared interests or experiences, like living in the same neighborhood or sharing a common religion. We participate in PTAs to build a new playground at our kid's school or join GoFundMe groups to cover the expenses of a neighbor who has a health crisis.

Of all the migrations from the physical to the digital world, perhaps the most important for us to understand is the migration of our communities. Just as in physical world communities, becoming a member of a virtual community doesn't always come with an obvious sign-up form. When I watch a video on YouTube about choosing what type of dog is good for a family with young children, I become part of the broader YouTube community, as well as a subcommunity of people who care about dog breeding. I may stay at the periphery by just watching watching videos or reading posts from others. But as I add comments, ask questions, or start to share content of my own, I become a more active member of that community.

Communities Need Shared Spaces

In 1989, sociologist Ray Oldenburg wrote *The Great Good Place: Cafes, Coffee Shops, Community Centers, Beauty Parlors, General Stores, Bars, Hangouts, and How They Get You Through the Day.*[1] In his book, Oldenburg talks about the necessity of having shared community spaces he calls "third places" (home and work being the other two). These third places are parks, shops, libraries, and any other space that allows us to come together and interact with other members of our various communities. Oldenburg maintains that third places are essential to host the communities that our functioning society depends on.

The digital world is chock-full of third places. They are the platforms that we all use to engage with others, including Facebook, YouTube, LinkedIn, Instagram, Goodreads, Wikipedia, Nextdoor, and Reddit. They also include thousands of topic-specific spaces like Buusu (language learning), DeviantArt (visual design), and Ravelry (knitting). And let's not forget our virtual mall—Amazon—where a huge community exists around discussing products (read the reviews of the "three wolf moon shirt" on Amazon if you want a fun example of that). Virtual community spaces are just as real and play just as important a role in our lives as their physical predecessors.

Author and entrepreneur Eli Pariser focuses on lessons we can learn from creating effective community spaces in the physical world to create effective community spaces in the virtual world. According to Pariser, successful physical community spaces require significant attention to three critical design elements: the functionality of the space, the quality of the programming that takes place there, and people who take ownership of the space to keep it welcoming and clean.

Pariser points out that as we've migrated our third places to the virtual world, we've spent our time focused on the first design element— the functionality that makes collaboration possible. We've created the tools to post and share content, create playlists, and "like" other people. But unlike physical shared spaces, we haven't focused nearly as much energy on improving the quality of content or identifying who is responsible for maintaining a safe and welcoming experience for people who participate in our online communities.

Becoming digital citizens means recognizing that our virtual spaces aren't just transactional websites, but community spaces that are critical to the ongoing health of our society and need to be cared for. It means understanding that the value of our virtual world isn't just entertainment, but the test kitchen for ideas that enrich our lives and improve the lives of those around us. As such, how we act and what we do in our virtual communities really matters. We need common agreement on certain behaviors that are expected of digital citizens and a concerted effort to teach and model those behaviors for our children if we hope to reduce our growing list of digital dysfunctions and create a virtual world they will be happy to grow up in.

Learning How to Act in Shared Spaces

Healthy communities always establish shared expectations for the behavior of their members. A church group may have an expectation of loving your neighbor as yourself. If you're a member of a soccer team, you agree to play by a certain set of rules, not only the written rules of the game, but also the unwritten rules of how you agree to engage with other members of the team—arrive on time for practices, tell the opposing team "good game" even when you lost, do what the coach asks of you in practice, and so on.

Our training for how to act in community spaces happens mostly informally by following the example of other community members, though there have certainly been explicit efforts to establish community norms in the physical world over the years. George Washington wrote *Rules of Civility and Decent Behavior in Company and Conversation* in 1746 based on a similar French work. His 110 guidelines aimed to instill norms of decency and appropriate manners for engaging in early third places. Emily Post also did her best, as did Miss Manners, in what nostalgically looks like a simpler, more forgiving time. The Bill of Rights establishes norms for the community of citizens of the United States. If you live in America, you are governed by the moral and political obligations of the contract.

We use a variety of strategies for communicating norms of our physical communities today as well. On a trip to London, I was met by a poster in an underground station teaching riders to "Help others off the train if they feel ill." Similarly, there are signs on all of the escalators at the Hong Kong International Airport telling travelers to "take care of children and the elderly." I saw this "sign-posting" strategy on a recent drive through Utah where a billboard with a picture of Mister Rogers, a legend for encouraging friendship, had the text "Friendship, pass it on!" Similar "pass it on" billboards have popped up across the country inviting us to serve others, overcome trials, and be healthy. The norms of my own neighborhood, like staying alert for crime, supporting the community swim team, and mowing my lawn in the summer, are communicated through town-hall-style meetings and newsletters. Parents and teachers spend a lot of time preparing young children for the behavioral norms of school. We teach kids to pay attention to the teacher, take turns at the playground, and be kind to kids who look or talk differently from us.

When we don't actively and continually teach behavioral expectations for shared community spaces, though, they fall apart. This is particularly challenging since the responsibility of maintaining the quality of shared spaces can always be justified as someone else's problem—what the British economist William Forster Lloyd called the "tragedy of the commons." In the 1800s, Lloyd observed farmers overgrazing animals on shared land, making it unusable for everyone, while carefully managing the amount of grazing on their own lands. When everybody is responsible for something, there is the risk that nobody is, to the detriment of everyone involved.

Viewing our online activity as participation in a virtual community, and not just the random surfing of websites, is a critically important first step to improving the quality of our life there. We should feel involvement and ownership as members of a given virtual community and be keenly aware of the tendency toward tragedy of our virtual commons. As we coach and prepare our children to be successful in the virtual spaces, we need to teach a set of norms and expectations for our behavior that are essential to bring the missing conscience to our digital world. We will explore them in detail starting in the next chapter.

Teaching Digital Norms in Digital Spaces

At this point, you might be wondering why I'm making such an effort to call out the differences between the physical world and the virtual world. Is it really necessary to distinguish between the two? And moreover, if we just teach our kids to be good humans, shouldn't that apply equally whether they are in virtual or physical spaces? Understanding the answer to these questions is fundamental to ensuring our children's digital well-being.

First, we have to understand a bit about how our brains work. To explain, as an illustration, I'll use the story of my friend Chris going to church. Chris actively participates in a lesson about being kind to his fellow beings. He holds the door while a young family slowly files past. On his way out, he stops to help an elderly lady down the steps to the parking lot, clearly demonstrating what he had been taught by the sermon. But as he's driving home, someone cuts him off a few blocks from his house. Chris honks and yells at the person who cut him off, clearly not in line with the lesson from church. What has happened here? Is this not the same man who held the door open and helped the lady down the stairs? Has he forgotten all of the lessons he just learned? Hardly. This example illustrates a phenomenon from research on human cognition: when our environment changes, it is harder to apply concepts learned from a different setting.

Learning in Different Contexts

Cognitive research has shown us that we learn most effectively when we are taught in the context where we will use the knowledge. Think back to a math class you had in high school or college. You learned as the teacher spoke, wrote things on a board, or assigned a worksheet. When you were tested, you were asked to demonstrate your knowledge in a very similar format to how you learned it—maybe the very same worksheet, but with some answers missing. With a bit of study, you were probably able to do a good job on the test. But if you were asked to apply the concepts in a real-world setting, you may have found that you struggled or didn't make the connection to use those math skills at all. Even though the underlying concept may have been the same, when the words were different or it was presented as a spoken versus written problem, knowing how to solve it became more difficult.

In fact, the concept of learning in the same context where you will need to perform has such a powerful effect that many schools are beginning to implement project-based learning, where they teach key concepts through simulated real-life events, not worksheets and written tests. It's the same reason airlines spend millions of dollars on simulators for their pilots to practice landing a plane safely in an emergency as opposed to taking a written test on how to do it. The closer you can mimic the environment where the skills are needed, the more likely recall will happen.

For this reason, it is important to make the distinction between the skills that we teach in the physical and virtual worlds. It's not reasonable to expect that our children will be able to translate the norms we teach them about their behavior in the physical world to the very different context of the digital world, if they've never had the chance to practice there. If we want our kids to be tolerant and kind in virtual spaces, we have to teach and model tolerance and kindness *in* those virtual spaces. We have to have open discussions and give them examples of what effective digital behavior looks like in our digital third places.

Fundamental Flaws in Our Approach to Teaching Digital Citizenship

In all this discussion, I would be remiss not to acknowledge that many efforts are already being made to teach young people how to operate online. Parents and teachers alike are growing increasingly aware of our digital dysfunctions, and they're starting to have these important conversations. But while well intentioned, there are two fundamental flaws that often show up in our current approach to teaching digital citizenship. I will point them out in the hope that we can join together to chart a better path forward.

More Than Online Safety

The first common error with our approach to teaching digital citizenship is overfocusing the conversation on online safety. We may be tempted to spend the majority of our time teaching skills like not sharing personal information online, not posting something they might regret later, or not talking to digital strangers. Teaching kids basic principles of online safety *is* important; in fact I consider it a key component of digital citizenship. But online safety is *just a fraction* of the skill set our kids need to thrive in today's virtual world. Online safety is a bit like the warning on the visor of the car that tells us to fasten our seatbelts. It's required; we do it before anything else, and we would be irresponsible to ignore it. But it's not where we spend the bulk of our energy when learning to be a safe driver. The vast majority of our energy is spent on the more complex skills that require practice, like how to read signs, properly control the car, and navigate to where we actually want to go.

As parents, we need to broaden the conversation beyond how to stay safe. Real digital well-being is about using technology to enrich our lives and make our communities better. It's about using technology to build healthy relationships with friends and family, and being able to quickly find the right sources of information to learn new things and make good decisions. It's about balancing our online and offline activities appropriately. These are life-enriching skills that go far beyond just being safe. As important as safety is, if we aren't able to articulate a broader, more meaningful vision for the use of tech to enrich our children's lives, there isn't much point in even teaching online safety in the first place; we could just resort to digging a hole in the backyard to bury our digital devices.

A List of "Dos," Not "Don'ts"

The second common error in our current approach to teaching digital citizenship is that much of what we teach is framed negatively. We tell kids all the things they *shouldn't* do: "Don't post where you live." "Don't look at inappropriate pictures." "Don't spend so much time on your phone." Don't, don't, don't. Teaching digital citizenship as a list of don'ts is misleading. Though well-intentioned, the "list of don'ts" approach may actually become a self-fulfilling prophecy. Here's an experiment. Try to not think of a small pink elephant. One with an umbrella in its trunk. The umbrella is open and decorated with panda bears. How are you doing at *not* thinking about what I'm describing to you in great detail?

My father attended a private religious school in the 1950s. Once a semester, the clerical leaders would give the students a list of all of the sins that they should never commit and a list of books they were not allowed to read. As my father recounts, the students took more diligent notes that day than they did the entire rest of the year, but not for the reasons the school leaders had hoped. The students were getting ideas for behaviors they had never considered and a reading list for summer vacation. When preparing youth for success online, there is a real risk in presenting a list of the things *not* to do, as it may become a list of ideas they had never considered before *we* planted them. This approach reinforces the bad without ever showing what the *good* looks like.

Another risk of the "don'ts" approach to teaching digital well-being is that you can't practice *not doing* something. Learning the skills of digital citizenship takes practice and happens over many years. Imagine if we tried to teach kids to play the piano by telling them all the ways to not do it correctly. To learn to play the piano, they have to first learn the names of the notes, then learn how to read music, and above all practice. The same is true with learning to become an effective digital citizen. (For another example, see "A Positive Approach for Preventing Cyberbullying" on the next page.)

Taking a negative approach to teaching digital citizenship is also problematic because it just isn't a very compelling message. In the 1980s, David Cooperrider and Suresh Srivastva, professors at Case Western Reserve University, conducted landmark research to make this point. They noticed that when trying to turn around struggling companies, traditional business consultants would identify all the things that were going wrong and present the leadership with a list of the problems they should fix. But Cooperrider and Srivastva found that they could actually get the companies to turn around faster by calling attention to the things that they were already doing right instead of the things that were wrong.[2] Their approach, which they called "appreciative inquiry," is now used by business consultants around the world. You can change behavior faster by doubling down on the positive aspects of good behavior than by spotlighting all of the bad things that should be stopped.

Finally, when it comes to setting the expectations for online behavior, whatever we teach our kids becomes the baseline that their

A Positive Approach for Preventing Cyberbullying

In reaction to rising cases of cyberbullying and teen suicides from horrible abuses online, there has been an uptick in teaching anti-cyberbullying in schools. While I'm glad that the education community recognizes the seriousness of this particular issue, anti-cyberbullying campaigns are a Band-Aid solution at best. For starters, we shouldn't wait until kids start getting bullied online to begin a conversation to try to stop it. We should be spending at least as much energy creating a virtual world where cyberbullying never starts in the first place. After all, that's what we do with other critical life skills. We don't teach anti-illiteracy; we teach kids to love reading. We don't teach anti-laziness; we model healthy exercise habits.

Instead of teaching anti-cyberbullying, we should teach what to do to prevent bullying in the first place: that the accepted norms of behavior in our virtual spaces include being kind and honest with others. And, yes, of course, when people don't live up to those norms, there are consequences because our digital community does not value other types of behavior.

behavior is anchored to. There will always be deviation from that baseline. Children will make some choices that exceed our expectations, and in other cases, their choices will fall short. But what we teach determines the starting point. If we start right at the "do not cross" line, we have no buffer before our kids enter truly destructive territory. Years ago a transportation company was interviewing new truck drivers. The route was dangerous and included traveling along many steep cliffs through a mountain pass. As the manager interviewed each applicant, he asked them, "How close can you drive to the

Let me share one example of a school that made the flip from a negative approach to teaching digital citizenship to a positive one. La Cañada is a National Blue Ribbon School outside of Los Angeles, serving approximately four thousand students every year. La Cañada's mission is to develop students who are uniquely prepared for the twenty-first century by focusing on the development of communication skills, creative problem-solving, and civic engagement. As they tried to make sure the students were prepared to be healthy technology users, district leaders Jennifer Zine and David Paszkiewicz realized they needed an approach that would give students opportunities to practice becoming contributing participants in virtual spaces. Instead of telling kids to stop cyberbullying, they began to teach how to be good online friends through their Building Cyber-Friendships initiative. They practice how to write thoughtful messages and recognize the importance of listening as well as posting in order to create meaningful online conversations. As students participate in the program, they explore different roles they can take in a digital space and learn how to recognize that their individual actions can have a positive impact on their friends and the broader online community.

edge of the cliff as you come around the mountain?" The first candidate replied that he was so skilled that he could drive within two feet of the edge. The second candidate bragged that he was so skilled that he could bring the tires within two inches of the edge of the road. The third and final candidate answered, "I drive as far away from the edge of the cliff as I possibly can." The third candidate was offered the job.

Describing the digital attributes we want our kids to embody places the starting point well within safe ground. Even when our kids make mistakes, they are still far away from the digital cliff. This doesn't mean that we can't ever define limits that can't be crossed, but if the majority of our energies are focused on defining and modeling the expected attributes of a healthy digital citizen, it will become the self-fulfilling prophecy.

A Once-in-a-Generation Window

Ensuring the success of our children and a more hopeful future digital world is reason enough to start a new conversation about how we are teaching digital citizenship. But there is a reason for additional urgency now: the increased access to internet connectivity in schools and at home.

While I was working for President Obama, one of my roles was to develop a National Ed Tech Plan—a vision and guide for how to use technology in schools.[3] When used effectively in schools, technology can be a powerful solution to many long-standing educational challenges. Through technology, schools that can't afford the latest textbooks can have access to the most up-to-date online resources. Schools in rural areas that often struggle to find highly qualified teachers can access expert teachers via Zoom. In one instance, a STEM school in Chattanooga, Tennessee, was able to remotely operate a $2 million scanning electron microscope located at the University of Southern California because both institutions were connected to the same high-speed network.[4]

As we were putting together the National Ed Tech Plan, though, we found that schools like the STEM school in Chattanooga were outliers. Most schools lacked the reliable internet connections needed to use any tech for learning. A teacher in South Carolina drove home this point most memorably. I had been invited by the Horry County school district to share some of the ways that technology could make learning more engaging for students. The group of teachers assembled listened patiently as I shared examples of schools like Chattanooga that were transforming learning through the smart use of tech. When I finished, a teacher in the back of the room raised her hand and asked me if I had "ever tried to drink peanut butter from a straw?" Before I could ask what she meant, she explained that drinking peanut butter from a straw was what it felt like to try to access the internet from her classroom. The room erupted in applause.

Upon returning to Washington, DC, our team discovered that despite our claims that the United States was among the first countries to have 100 percent of schools connected to the internet, most teachers did not have working internet in their classrooms. It turned out that if any part of the school building had an internet connection, the school was classified as a "connected school." So, what we had really accomplished was connecting 100 percent of school *offices* to the internet, and sometimes a computer lab or library along the way. Under the direction of the president and secretary of education, we redefined what it meant to be a connected school (to include having broadband Wi-Fi in all classrooms). With the support of education nonprofits, corporate leaders, education researchers, politicians from both sides of the aisle, and teachers from schools across the country, we redesigned an FCC program to help subsidize the cost of internet to schools. Within three years, the United States went from 15 percent connected classrooms to 98 percent of schools with access to broadband Wi-Fi in the classroom.

Other countries have followed a similar path to prioritizing connectivity for students. Combine those efforts with the increased connectivity at home in the wake of Covid-19 online learning, and we find our children with unprecedented access to connectivity at home and at school. This opportunity gives us a unique window to rethink how we're teaching our kids about what kind of people they want to be in a virtual space before existing habits become their norm. It's an opportunity to set new guidelines and new expectations. It's an opportunity to talk about more than just online safety. And it's an opportunity to make the conversation positive. That's the good news. The bad news is that not nearly enough attention has been given to having this discussion. We can't address the problem by simply adding another class to the school day. This is about creating a digital *culture* at home and at school. And this unique window that we've been given will soon close. If we choose not to reset expectations, our existing haphazard norms will continue, and we will have lost a once-in-a-generation opportunity to rethink how we are preparing the next generation of digital citizens.

Starting a New Conversation

We cannot afford to be haphazard in our approach to teaching digital citizenship. Along with the recent increase in connectivity in our homes and schools, we have been handed a unique opportunity to examine our digital culture. Our conversation needs to be broader than just online safety and should focus on positive attributes that our kids can emulate and practice and, in so doing, improve our communities and build healthy virtual relationships. In the next chapters, we will explore five attributes that should guide our approach to teaching digital well-being:

Balanced. Balanced digital citizens participate in a variety of online activities and make informed decisions about how to prioritize their time in virtual and physical spaces.

Informed. Informed digital citizens evaluate the accuracy, perspective, and validity of digital media and have developed critical skills of curating information from the digital world.

Inclusive. Inclusive digital citizens are open to hearing and recognizing multiple viewpoints and engaging with others online with respect and empathy.

Engaged. Engaged digital citizens use technology and digital channels to solve problems and be a force for good in their physical and virtual communities.

Alert. Alert digital citizens are aware of their digital actions and know how to be safe and create safe spaces for others online.

As we explore this framework, I will draw comparisons between familiar parenting and teaching concepts from the physical world to help successfully navigate parenting and teaching in the digital world. For each attribute, I will give conversation starters and practical strategies for building them into the culture of our homes and schools. In so doing, we can choose to focus technology's accelerating forces on improving our world and deepening our humanity.

The task of keeping up with all the potential virtual spaces where our children may be involved can seem daunting. But like most of our digital citizenship conversations, this gets easier as we apply these same five attributes to our own digital habits and spend time understanding what our children are experiencing. As parents, we can familiarize ourselves with locations like TikTok, Snapchat, Discord, or Instagram, so we understand the context of their digital communities. We can talk with our children about where they're going online and what they're doing there, asking questions just as we would if we were asking about a party they were going to or which friends they were hanging out with on a Saturday afternoon. This book will help you have these conversations, prepare your children for how to respond if they ever feel unsafe online, and teach them to be a force for good in the digital world.

As Eli Pariser puts it, if online digital spaces are going to be our new home, let's make them a comfortable, beautiful place to live. A place we all feel some ownership of. A place where we get to know each other. A place we'd actually want to visit and bring our kids.

3

Balanced

Using Technology on Our Terms

A n important rite of passage for parents and children alike is learning (and teaching) how to ride a bike. For generations, we all used essentially the same approach: training wheels. Those rickety little wheels provided a safe way for kids to get used to riding the bike before having to do it on their own. The problem is that those well-intentioned training wheels actually taught the wrong skills. Driving and steering aren't nearly as important as learning to balance. So inevitably there came that heart-stopping moment of taking the wheels off and running behind your totally out-of-control kid, hoping nobody ended up in the hospital. Even if it didn't result in any broken bones, the process took longer than it needed to, and the transition was always more difficult than necessary.

Then along came a totally crazy new idea, a small bike with *no pedals*. Balance bikes, as they are known, help kids learn to tackle the most important part of riding a bike (balancing and counter-steering) first and the least important part (using the pedals) later, with an approach that is immediately transferable. There was no heart-attack moment for my kids, who used balance bikes. When it was time to switch to a real bike, they just got on and rode off. It was amazing. How could we ever have taught kids to ride a bike any other way?

When teaching kids to regulate the amount of tech use in their lives, we are still taking a training-wheels approach. It is inefficient and ineffective, but familiar. But like learning to ride a bike, our approach to teaching kids to regulate their device use needs to change. We need a strategy aligned to the bigger picture of what we're trying to accomplish in both our physical and digital worlds *with* those devices. There is a better way.

We've Outgrown Screen Time

Keeping the previous example in mind, let's discuss the idea of screen time. One of the most common questions parents ask me is how much screen time is appropriate for their kid on a given day. I understand why they ask this question and appreciate the intent behind it: parents recognize that there should be limits on digital activities. We've all seen how addictive certain apps can be. We've watched children (other people's, of course) actually walk into walls because they are too glued to their screens to look where they are going. We've all read the mommy-blog posts about the dangers of too much tech use. We know there must be limits. Yet, at the same time, there are lots of enriching activities that our children can do online. Not to mention, appropriate tech use is fun. The privilege of participating in digital activities can be a great motivating factor to get other jobs done too. And let's face it, children participating in healthy digital activities can provide a much-needed break for parents that is also safe. If you're the type of parent who plans a nurturing activity for your kids every second of the day, you can absolutely feel free to judge what I'm about to say. But the reality is that technology has been a key strategy in keeping sanity in our house when I need to make dinner or we need to take *another* trip to the store because I forgot something on the list.

We all live with these competing realities: on one hand, technology is useful and fun for our kids, and on the other, we don't want kids walking into walls or having their brains turn to mush. So, we turn to the clock as a way to mediate these competing concerns. If we can just set a reasonable time limit, everything will be OK. However, as I will show, using the clock as the primary way to set boundaries is misdirected vigilance, like training wheels, and is not the best long-term approach to raising healthy digital kids.

Based on Old Research

The idea of limiting tech use based primarily on the amount of *time* a child spends on a screen each day stems from research conducted on children watching television. Excessive television consumption in children was correlated with adverse effects on their health in terms of weight, sleep habits, and language development. Studies showed that fast-paced cartoon television shows could have a negative impact on cognitive skills including problem-solving, working memory, and inhibitory control in young children.[1] Based on these and similar studies on TV use, the American Academy of Pediatrics (AAP) previously recommended limiting screen time for children to two hours per day. It reasoned that any device with a screen was analogous to the TV experience.

But TV and mobile computing devices are not the same. Most notably, television is an entirely passive experience. There is no way for TV shows to engage with the watchers. A few kids' shows (think *Dora the Explorer* or *Bo on the Go!*) ask kids questions as part of the show and even pause for them to answer. But kids rarely take the bait. TV watchers can fall asleep or slip into a coma, and the TV continues playing its programs without missing a beat. Yes, it's true that other tech devices can be put into "TV mode" by using apps like Netflix or Disney+, but the majority of the activities that can be performed on a mobile device have some level of two-way interaction, either because of a connection to another human through the device or from computer-generated responses based on the choices of the user. Applying research conclusions from the passive TV experience to highly interactive tech use is a bit like giving someone medication for a sickness that someone else has. As a result, in 2016, the AAP revised its guidelines, removing specific time limitations for children ages six and up.[2] The US Department of Education echoed this guidance.[3] The World Health Organization more recently published guidelines placing screen-time limitations only on what it called "*sedentary* screen time" (watching TV or digital activities with limited or no interaction).[4]

Reinforces Binary Thinking

Another problem with using screen time as the primary approach for moderating tech use is that it creates the perception that all activities that take place in the digital world are of equal value. Nothing could be further from the truth. I think we can agree that FaceTiming with Grandma and playing *Temple Run* are activities with *very* different value, even though both occur on the same device. Even among games we see different value from different apps. *Candy Crush* and *Minecraft* are both games, but one requires about as much creative thinking as a slot machine, and the other is a highly creative design platform. If you've never heard of *Minecraft*, think of it like a digital version of Legos, but with unlimited pieces and the ability to program new types of interactions (you can actually build a working computer in *Minecraft*).

The point is that when we moderate device use by screen time, we are also communicating that tech use is binary, allowed or not. If that is the case, a young person will likely draw the conclusion that all the activities available on their device during that time are of the same value. This removes the necessity to develop the critical skill of learning to associate different values with different digital activities. To underscore this point, imagine for a moment that we are talking about teaching our kids to become healthy eaters. Just because it is "food time" (aka dinner) doesn't mean that eating Twinkies is an appropriate meal. In our house, you are allowed to eat fruit and drink water anytime, day or night, if you are hungry or thirsty. A variety of other foods become available at lunch and dinner. Sometimes we break out the chips or have a Twinkie for a snack, but we teach that foods like chips and Twinkies have little nutritional value and should be eaten far less often than fruits and vegetables, and only when other healthy food is also being eaten that day. The goal is to teach our kids that they should eat different types of foods in different amounts if they are going to have a balanced diet. When it comes to device use, the idea that our kids should consume different digital activities in differing amounts based on their value is an equally important concept.

Limits the Ability to Self-Regulate

Finally, using screen time as the primary factor for moderating tech use takes away our children's ability to learn to self-regulate. Waiting for a timer to tell us when to be done may work for the bumper car ride at an amusement park, but it is not a good strategy to navigate the expressways of the digital world. We want our kids to learn to move on to new activities when it is appropriate to do so, not just because a timer runs out. The danger of teaching kids to stop using technology only when the timer goes off is that it prevents them from developing the "muscles" of regulating their own amount of participation in digital activities. What will happen on the day when no time limit is given?

Let's go back to the food analogy. The goal is not to eat nonstop until the lunch or dinner hour is over. The goal is to recognize when we've eaten enough, even if there is still a little food left on our plate. Remember, even healthy food, if we aren't learning to self-regulate, becomes unhealthy. I could probably eat twelve apples during the course of my lunch hour, but if I did, I'd be very sick. Likewise, it would be unhealthy to believe that my cue to stop eating apples should come only from a timer telling me that the lunch hour is over, instead of from my body recognizing that I'm full. A critical skill for budding digital citizens is learning to recognize for themselves when it's time to transition to another digital or physical activity.

At this point, you might be thinking I'm making the case that there should be no limits on technology use. Nothing could be further from the truth. We need appropriate limits, but there are better approaches to finding them than measuring screen time. Let's explore a more effective approach to teach limits that is in line with the US Department of Education's and the World Health Organization's updated guidelines.

A Better Approach: Finding Balance

If we've outgrown using screen time as our tool for moderating tech use in our families, how do we avoid having a wall-crashing kid? Instead of enforcing screen-time limits, the concept that we should seek to teach is *balance*. This is a concept that we regularly teach in the physical world. We point out that healthy people balance the time they spend with friends and family, and by themselves. They know how to balance exercise and rest. They make time for work and play, being serious and having fun. In school, we reinforce these concepts from the first days of kindergarten. We have math and language arts, but we also value music and physical education. We study for tests, but we also play during recess. Being a healthy person in the physical world means learning how to have moderation in all things. While some activities can be easily classified as either good (brushing your teeth) or bad (picking a fight with your brother), the value of the vast majority of activities is determined by their proportional relationship to other activities. Exercise is a good thing, unless we start exercising so much that we aren't finishing our homework or spending time with family and friends. Getting rest is also good, but oversleeping, especially habitually, diminishes our productivity and mental health. Being imaginative is good, but when done in the wrong contexts, it's considered lying.

Balance may not look the same from day to day either. The day before a big science project is due, it would be out of balance to spend the whole day riding a bike. The day before a violin recital, it might be inappropriate to spend the whole day reading instead of practicing, even though on a different day that might be a great choice. As parents, we watch for indicators in the physical world when activities feel out of balance. Finding balance in our virtual world is just as important. We have to make sure we are equally adamant about helping our kids learn to find *digital* balance as we are at helping them find balance in other parts of their lives. The following three principles can help.

Principle 1: Experience a Variety of Digital Activities

When creating the US National Ed Tech Plan, my team began by looking at the digital divide—the gap between kids who had access to technology and those who didn't.[5] Earlier in this book I explained how that work led to providing connectivity for underresourced and rural schools. But our work at the US Department of Education also revealed another digital divide that hasn't received nearly as much attention. In the schools we visited, we began noticing two types of technology use. In some classrooms, students were using technology in a very active way: creating and designing, collaborating and problem-solving. In others, students were using technology in a very passive way: watching content online. The only interactivity the second group of students had was clicking the "next" button to advance a slide or answer a multiple-choice quiz at the end of the unit. In the National Ed Tech Plan, we called this gap the "digital *use* divide." Students who were taught to use technology as a creation or problem-solving tool were on the active side of the divide. Students who primarily used technology as a content-consumption tool were on the passive side of the divide. For the passive users, technology was very similar to a portable TV. For the active technology users, their device was more analogous to a set of paintbrushes or building blocks. The exact same devices could lead to a very different experience, based on the activities that students were conducting on them.

As parents, it is important to help expand our kids' digital palate by exposing them to the wide variety of activities that exist in the virtual world. We shouldn't be satisfied with just the apps and digital activities that our kids already know about, any more than we should allow our kids to only try the foods they ask for. (If that were the case in my house, we would be eating macaroni and cheese for every meal.) If you find your kid is requesting the same types of apps (for example, eight different variations of a first-person shooter game), you might agree to approve the next new app if they also find an app to try that is in a different category (for example, a rhythm game or photo-editing app). Even if they don't use those new apps as often, just the process of searching for different types of apps increases kids' awareness of new possibilities.

Another way to help expand the range of digital activities is to periodically suggest new apps for our kids to try, just as we period-ically suggest a new book for them to read. I am constantly looking for books that I think my kids will like. Sometimes I get it right, and other times I don't, but either way, this communicates that the things they choose to read matter to me. If we don't ever recommend new apps to our children to try, then we can't really be too frustrated if we don't like the digital media they choose on their own. This, of course, means that as parents, we ourselves have to be aware of different types of digital activities. There are many ways to do this. Sites like Com-mon Sense Media or the EdSurge app index provide expert reviews of apps specifically with children's use in mind. I particularly like digital tools that encourage kids to develop their creative talents, like making movies or composing music, as they help reinforce the idea that tech-nology is most powerful when it is used to assist humans in design and problem-solving process. In chapter 6, I will provide examples of digital activities focused on helping kids become more engaged with their communities and families.

Be aware that the idea of participating in a variety of digital activities runs directly against the design of some apps. Apps with in-app purchases or advertisements are often designed intentionally to keep young people using that specific app as long as humanly possible. Using tools like autoscroll, streaks, and point systems, they try to make it as uncomfortable as possible for the user to switch to a different digital activity. It's not evil for an app developer to design an app to be as attractive as possible, but it is problematic if we don't alert our kids to what is really going on. As we teach digital balance, it's helpful to call out these design elements and explain that their purpose is to limit the range of digital activities we participate in. For example, if there is a game where the player loses all of their points if they don't play every day, we might explain that the person who designed that game is using a trick (called a streak) to keep players from using their devices for other activities. If there is an app that unlocks special features when players download other apps by the same developer, we might point out that the designer is using a trick to get them to buy their other apps. It doesn't mean our kids can't still choose to use these apps, but they should do so being fully aware of the techniques the app developer employs to undermine digital balance.

Principle 2: Recognize the Varying Values of Digital Activities

Having exposure to a range of digital activities is important in the same way that having fresh fruits and vegetables at home is essential to becoming a healthy eater. But just putting broccoli on the counter may not be enough to motivate most kids to start eating vegetables. We also have to explicitly teach the concept that different foods have differing levels of benefit to our bodies. When teaching digital balance, one of the most important skills we can teach our kids is to ask how much value they receive for the digital activities they are participating in.

For older kids, we might teach this concept using an analogy known as attention economics, based on work by business strategists Thomas Davenport and John Beck in the early 2000s.[6] Their idea is that in a world of unlimited competing digital resources, our attention has actual monetary value. In other words, attention economics takes the term "paying attention" literally. We are making choices about how to distribute deposits of our valuable attention among competing activities. Using attention economics to explain digital balance might start with a tangible example from the physical world. Something like: "If someone asked to buy your bike for $5, would you sell it?" Why not? Because the value of the bike is much greater than the $5 they would be giving you. From there, we can introduce the idea that our attention has value, too. We can talk about how much we have "paid" in our attention to different activities during the day. This becomes a fun way to calculate how much time and creative energy we're spending on our digital activities. But most importantly, it allows us to ask if the activities we're paying for with our attention are giving us a reasonable return for our investment. Did the $10 of my attention I just paid to playing *Among Us* return a value that was reasonable? What if I had spent that same amount of my attention playing a different game, or using Marco Polo to talk with a friend? This can help kids begin to see that their attention has real value, and they should expect a return of equivalent value from their digital activities.

For younger kids, the idea of attention economics might be too abstract to understand. But there are other ways to teach the idea that different digital activities have different values associated with them. On Sunday afternoons, our family has a block of free time between church in the morning and dinner in the evening. We've made a conscious decision to take a break from doing all schoolwork on Sundays so our kids can have a day to reset. But we also found that without some structure, our well-intentioned Sunday family time quickly turns into fight-with-your-brothers-all-afternoon time (shoot me now). So, together with our kids, we created a list of low-, neutral-, and high-bar

Sunday activities. We assigned values to them and wrote them on a chart. For this list, we included both physical world and digital activities, but to illustrate my point here, I'm only including the digital ones. Low-bar activities were things like watching *National Geographic* videos, listening to music, or playing *Minecraft*. Medium-bar activities included things like playing a chess app with a sibling, reading an ebook, or listening to a podcast. High-bar activities included writing a letter to a friend, FaceTiming with a grandparent, learning new words in Duolingo, or composing a song in GarageBand. Medium- or high-bar activities could be done at any time. But high-bar activities could also offset low-bar activities. So, if one of our children wanted to play *Minecraft*, they could earn that opportunity by writing a message to Grandma or composing a song. This helps reinforce the concept that different digital activities have different values—a fundamental part of learning balance in the virtual world.

Principle 3: Adapt to the Interests and Needs of Each Child

The third principle of teaching balance comes from recognizing the unique needs of each child. We cannot apply a single formula for balanced tech use to all children any more than we can give a single prescription for everyone needing glasses. When considering the appropriate balance of amount and type of digital activities, we need to consider the child's natural interests. Talk with them about how well their digital activities support their goals and interests. Ask which types of activities would be a stretch for them to complete and which wouldn't. Getting my son to read a chapter of an ebook is a big stretch that we might reward with an opportunity to play a game in order to keep good balance. For my daughter, reading the ebook would *be* the reward.

Ask yourself similar questions about the design of varying digital activities as you seek to find the right balance. For example, consider how appropriate a particular app or online community is, given the child's age or maturity level. Or if participation in a particular digital activity makes sense based on their other responsibilities. The answer will be different based on current school deadlines or extracurricular demands. It will likely vary between summer and the school year as well. There are a variety of unusual factors that could change the appropriate balance on a given day, such as physical illness, severe weather, or extended travel. If a child is sick in bed or stuck in a car on a long trip, the balance for what digital activities are appropriate could change. Finally, consider how much parental supervision is possible. Making a movie is a great digital activity if you are available to guide and support but might be too challenging for younger kids to do on their own. While at least some digital activities should be shared with parents, the amount of parental involvement that is possible may shape the balance of activities. Consider and discuss all these factors with your children as you work to find the right balance on their digital menu.

Resetting Language

My wife and I often find ourselves repeating the same things to our kids over and over again. In fact, we have an ongoing joke that you could replace us with a tape recorder and our kids would never know the difference. At one point, we actually started to write down our most common messages: "Don't forget to wash your hands"—that's recording #15. "Please shut off the light when you leave the room"—that's recording #37. "Does everyone have their seatbelts on?"—that's #54, and so on. If we were to compile all parent recordings, we would find a whole category of statements just focused on technology use. Many are based on the screen-time paradigm.

After years of thinking about moderating tech use based on screen time, it can be difficult to shift toward making balance the goal. As such, some of our statements need rerecording, with our knowledge of digital balance in mind. Here are four common screen-time statements that I often hear parents make with suggestions for how we might reframe them as digital-balance statements instead. These may seem like minor language changes, but the way we talk to our kids about using technology can have a huge impact on their ability to become balanced digital citizens.

Reframe 1: "You're Addicted to Your Phone"

This statement may be the most common of all parent recordings. Saying "you're addicted to your phone" is a confusing message for a child. In most cases, it's not the device itself that is addictive, but a particular app or website that, when used continually, can create imbalance or even addiction. In order to reframe that statement, we should state what the real concern is. Is the problem that the child is not participating in physical-world activities that we think are important? If so, instead of communicating that we have a problem with the amount of time our kid is using a device, we could reframe with a compelling reason to do something *else*. The reframing of this statement would call out the imbalance between digital and physical world activities and give examples of specific physical-world activities that might not be getting enough priority. The reframed statement might sound something like: "It doesn't seem like you've gotten any exercise yet today" or "I noticed you haven't spent any time with your family since you've gotten home from school; let's do that for a bit so we can balance out how you spend your day."

Reframe 2: "You've Been Playing That Game for Too Long"

The second statement, "You've been playing [insert game here] for too long," also reinforces a screen-time mentality. It focuses on the amount of time our kids are spending on a single digital activity. This statement is problematic because it doesn't focus on what is wrong with the activity. Kids might even notice that if they were watching a movie (also on a screen) for the same two hours, we probably wouldn't say anything at all. The digital balance reframe would require us to evaluate the qualities of the game. If we feel the value of the game is less than the value of other digital activities, we might call that out. The reframed statement might sound something like, "It seems like this game is getting more of your attention than it deserves, given the fact that it's mostly based on repetition and luck." It might lead to a conversation about the value of different types of apps that are installed on the device and whether they might give a better return on the invested attention. We might ask something like, "What other digital activities do you want to do with the time you spend on your phone today?"

Reframe 3: "Stop Sitting Around on the Computer All Day"

"Stop sitting around on the computer all day" is another statement that sends a confusing message, especially if the suggestion for a replacement activity is to read a book instead. Reading a book, it turns out, is even less active than using a device. I'm not saying that reading a book isn't a good activity for a kid to find balance in that moment. It's just that the *reason* given ("stop sitting around") makes no sense to a kid who is offered an alternative activity that involves just as much sitting around. Also, it is entirely possible that the kid was reading on their device in the first place. As we use the balance reframe here, we need to be specific about the activity we feel is out of balance. If the concern is that they're not spending enough time reading, that's a great conversation to have. We might discuss the importance of making sure there is reading time (on or off a device) at some point during each day. If on the other hand our concern is a need for physical activity, that is a different balance conversation. In that case the reframe would be less about not using the computer and more about finding an appropriate time to go for a bike ride or a run.

Reframe 4: "You Need to Interact with Real People"

Telling a kid to "get off your phone to spend time with people" is a statement that makes no sense to someone who is engaging with *more* people through their phone than they are when they're off the phone. As already discussed, one of the main advantages to participation in the virtual world is that it allows us to interact with a greater variety of people than we could in the physical world alone. Once again, the reframe requires us to first ask ourselves what feels out of balance. A possible balance reframe here might be "Your family wants a chance to spend some time with you as well" or "It's good to have some in-person interactions with your friends, too." That might lead to a conversation about the right balance between interacting with friends and family virtually versus in person.

Yes, They Still Sell Alarm Clocks

There is one particular concern that seems most problematic when talking to parents about finding digital balance: sleep. According to both American Academy of Sleep Medicine and the National Sleep Foundation, school-aged children should get between nine and twelve hours and teenagers between eight and ten hours of sleep a night.[7] Not getting enough sleep leads to a host of problems, including a decreased ability to regulate mood and emotion, an increased emergence of depression, and an increased risk of obesity.[8] Sleep deprivation leads to an alcoholic-intoxication-level dulling of cognitive and motor function.[9] Not only does chronic sleep deprivation lead to increasingly risky decision-making, it also impairs people's ability to realize that their decisions have become riskier.[10] There is also an important connection between sleep and memory as our daily experiences are consolidated into longer-term memories while we sleep. It's a bit like downloading all of our activity for a day into a file that can be retrieved in the future.[11] If we don't get adequate sleep, the download never really happens.

When our technology use is out of balance, sleep is one of the first things to be impacted. According to Dr. Lauren Hale and a team of medical researchers, three-fourths of US children and adolescents report sleeping with a digital device. Most of them also report regular use of these devices during the hour before bedtime.[12] This leads them to get almost an hour less sleep per night and poorer quality sleep, as compared with kids who don't sleep with devices in or next to their beds.[13] Even if they aren't using their phones before sleeping, constant overnight notifications can impact their sleep. Over a third of teens report getting up at least once in the middle of the night to check for something on their phone other than the time.[14]

Digital platforms have a financial motivation to keep us from sleeping. Reed Hastings, CEO of Netflix, once said the biggest competitor to the Netflix streaming video service is not other media companies, but sleep. Once you're asleep, you are no longer viewing the content (and advertising) of digital products. In case there is any confusion, Hastings added, "and we're winning!"[15]

As I talk to parents, one of the reasons I hear over and over as to why their kids sleep with their devices is that they use them as alarm clocks. Fortunately, I tell them, an exciting technology can completely solve this problem and costs about as much as a cup of Starbucks coffee. It's called an alarm clock. It works just like the alarm on a phone but doesn't do anything else that would distract from sleeping. If you haven't done so already, please go buy your kid an alarm clock and stop letting them sleep with their phones. Ironically, Facebook CEO Mark Zuckerberg knows the importance of screen-free bedtime better than most. When his wife, Priscilla, who is a pediatrician, was having trouble sleeping, Zuckerberg custom designed a screenless alarm clock that told her when it was time to get up by displaying a soft light.[16]

As parents, we need to develop family norms to ensure devices are not next to young people when they should be sleeping. As a family, you could designate a power-off time when everyone agrees to turn off their devices. Or you could designate a spot in the kitchen where all devices go to sleep at night. To reinforce this concept at our house, my wife and I hold a strategic monopoly on all device charging. We have only one charging station; it's on a table in our bedroom (away from our bed). We offer free device-charging service every night, as long as the devices are turned off and plugged in before we go to sleep. If a device is not at the charging station by 10:00 p.m., we happily offer our charging services for the next day, but our daytime charging service takes the entire day. Funny how that works.

Taking a Break Isn't a Punishment

One of the easiest strategies for teaching digital balance is to help kids become accustomed to occasionally taking device breaks. I've watched many kids who only have their devices taken away as a punishment. This perversely reinforces the idea that it's a bad thing to ever be without their devices. Balanced digital citizens understand that at times it's healthy to choose not to participate in digital activities. The language of "taking a break" is a helpful concept to practice. Occasionally we might say, "You haven't done anything wrong, but let's take a phone break for the afternoon." Our kids have learned that when this happens, they're not in trouble. We're just helping them rebalance. It's true that device breaks might mean that our kids may even be bored. Manoush Zomorodi has studied the surprising connection between boredom and creativity and play. In her book *Bored and Brilliant*, she explains the neurological factors that limit creativity in children who don't ever experience boredom. So, if a break from a device leads to a bit of boredom, realize that it may actually increase your child's creativity.

We can also schedule screen-free moments into our daily routines. Many families are now adopting "device-free meals" (Common Sense Media created a hilarious campaign for device-free meals with Will Ferrell that you should take a minute to watch). Having device-free meals means we leave all devices in a place away from the table (and turn the TV off) before sitting down for dinner. Everyone in the family participates, including the adults, which can be much more difficult than for the children. After about two weeks, it will become a habit, and it will feel very weird to have meals any other way. Other options include picking a day of the week to take a break from phones (for example, device-free Tuesday) or taking a periodic "social media fast" when the whole family logs off all their social media for a week. These activities all reinforce the concept that it's OK to periodically take a break from our digital world activities in order to keep balance in our lives.

Evaluating Apps

Being a balanced digital citizen, and the parent of one, means learning how to decide which apps to permit on devices. Before sharing some strategies for doing this, let me call out a strategy that is *not* an effective way for making the decision: looking at what other kids are doing. Unfortunately, this is a fairly common way that parents decide which apps they will permit. The number of kids who supposedly already have [insert app name here] is rarely a compelling reason to install it on our own kids' phones. Not only is that logic a risky way to make any decision, but the data used is always entirely skewed in the kids' favor.

One of my kids recently made the case to convince me to approve TikTok on her phone. In her mind, she was the only person in her school who didn't already have TikTok (a horrifying oversight, I'm sure). The reality, which I knew from talking to other parents, was that many other kids did not have access to TikTok. While you should certainly be aware when your child's perception might not match reality, the more important point here is that the number of other kids with (or without) access to an app is almost never a good reason for us to approve the app for our kids.

How many kids have TikTok on their phones

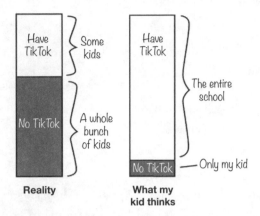

A better approach to choosing apps might be to have kids learn to pitch us on an app they'd like to have. This is not the same as begging or even asking. Pitching an app is making the case for why it should be approved based on some agreed-upon criteria. These don't have to be overly complicated guidelines, just some basic questions to consider. Joseph South, chief learning officer at the International Society for Technology in Education, says that as a parent, he teaches his kids to evaluate apps based on the following questions:

- How does the app connect me to other people? (Who are the people, are they people I know in person, and what kinds of interactions does this app allow?)

- How does the app make money? (Through ads, in-app purchases, up-front payment, etc.)

- How does the app keep me engaged? (Through quality content, habit-inducing measures, etc.)

- How does this app handle the issue of privacy? (What information about me does the app require up front, and what are the terms of service that relate to privacy?)

- Does this app make sense for me? (Based on things like age, disposition, ability and willingness to assess risk, ability to self-regulate, etc.)

- What do credible third-party reviewers say about the app?

When kids know we are going to ask those questions, they will learn to come to us with the answers ready as part of their pitch. This approach takes the parent out of the bad-cop role. When they request a new app, together you can discuss whether the app meets your criteria. If it doesn't, then it wasn't a mean parent who denied the app, but instead you both agreed the app simply didn't measure up to the criteria. This creates a much healthier relationship and puts parents and kids on the same team. It's not personal; sometimes apps just don't meet the threshold.

More importantly, pitching apps sets up healthy, long-term digital citizenship behavior. The process of pitching an app to a parent is the exact same skill we want kids to learn for themselves when they are older (instead of pitching to a parent, they will be answering those same questions for themselves). As part of the pitch, a kid might identify that a particular app might need careful monitoring because it has some elements with the potential to interfere with their digital balance. In that case, it might make sense to check back after a week of using the app to reevaluate it together. There are certain apps that are only appropriate when other activities aren't available, like during a long car ride. If you have children who already have devices loaded with apps, make time to review and evaluate whether the apps should stay or go.

Renee Hobbs, a respected researcher on media literacy education, recommends that parents spend time in digital spaces with their children. The purpose of this time is not to control their behavior, but to mentor them in navigating those spaces safely and effectively. We can help children evaluate their presence in that space and determine if it's where they really want to be. This also helps parents gain a better understanding about what online activities kids most enjoy, which can help suggest other types of digital activities.

Device-Use Agreements

Setting expectations for device use with children and youth is a key part of creating a healthy digital culture at home and school. Creating device agreements is an easy way to align device use with the culture you're trying to create. A device-use agreement is simply a document that explains how and when a child should use digital devices. It may also explain what privileges may be added if the child uses devices consistently according to the agreement as well as consequences when they do not meet expectations.

Keep these three things in mind when creating a device-use agreement:

1. ***Keep it positive.*** It can be tempting to fall back into the mode of making a list of "don'ts." (You might even reread chapter 2 before writing the agreement.)

2. ***Write in plain English.*** This isn't a real estate contract or a piece of legislation; write it as you would say it to the child.

3. ***Involve your kids.*** As you come up with the expectations, allow them to have input, make suggestions, and ask questions.

A sample device use agreement, based on the ones we use with our family, is provided at the end of this chapter. We chose items to include in the agreement to support the digital culture my wife and I we wanted to create. For example, family mealtimes are an important part of our family culture, so the agreement includes taking a device break during mealtimes. The agreement should be tailored to the needs of each child as well, which will depend on age, maturity, areas of interest, and so on. We wrote this agreement when our daughter first got a phone with a data plan. For that reason, there are expectations, such as needing to request permission before sending a picture, that might not be necessary for someone who has already been using a phone responsibly for several years. Device-use agreements should be updated periodically (I'd recommend doing it yearly on a birthday or the start of school) as devices change and young people become more experienced digital citizens.

Device-use agreements, either at home or at school, are learning tools, not legal entrapments. Some of the best learning opportunities come when your child has done something that goes against the principles of the agreement and you both get to practice how to resolve it when the stakes are low. You want to encourage them to talk with you about it when something goes wrong. This habit is critical to develop so they feel comfortable coming to you, should they ever have a more serious problem online in the future.

You should take violations of the agreement seriously, but the consequence should not inhibit the child from wanting to talk to you in the future. When our daughter sent a picture to someone without permission for the first time, we simply reminded her of the agreement and thanked her for telling us. The second time it happened, we discussed with her why this was an important part of the agreement and decided together to take a break from the phone for a couple of days. We didn't punish but just reminded her of the importance of demonstrating trustworthy digital behavior. As soon as this was no longer an issue—and as she got older—that part of the agreement was changed to "be responsible with what pictures you share," allowing her to share pictures without asking permission each time. The idea is to look for consistency over time, not freak out over a single incident that goes wrong. Remember to express appreciation when your child consistently meets the expectations of the agreement as well.

In our family, if our children tell us that they have broken a part of the agreement, they know it will result in a minor consequence. If they don't come to us and we discover it later, the consequence becomes more severe. They quickly learn it's much better to talk with us right away when some part of their digital behavior is out of line with the agreement.

As parents we know that if we're not careful, certain digital activities can consume more of our children's time and focus than they

Sample Device-Use Agreement

Using your device is a privilege. With any privilege comes responsibility. Here are the expectations for using your device:

When is it OK to use your device?

- You need to finish your jobs before using your phone (other than texting your parents).
- At mealtimes, your phone needs to take a rest in another room.
- If you are using your phone in any room, the door needs to stay open.
- Devices get brought to the charging station by 10:00 every night.

What should you do with your device?

- Help us capture family memories (take photos of places we visit, record family stories, etc.).
- Use your phone to help you learn (doing homework, working on school projects, and learning how to do new things).
- Have fun (read, play fun games, listen to good music).

Who should you interact with?

- Stay in touch with your friends and family members (talk to your cousins, grandparents, etc.).
- Let Mom or Dad know the first time you want to send a message to a new contact who is not a member of our extended family.
- Ask Mom or Dad before sending a picture/video to anyone.

The things you do on your device are not secret. Mom and Dad have the right to look at anything on your phone. If you change your password, you need to let us know what it is. If you decide that you need a phone break, you can bring us your phone to hold onto for a bit. We may also decide that you need to take a phone break from time to time. That's not a punishment, just a break.

We all make mistakes. When you do something with your device that is not in line with this agreement, let us know and we'll help you figure out how to make it right. Over time, as you demonstrate your ability to keep the principles of this agreement, additional device privileges will be provided. If you are not able to consistently keep your part of this agreement, existing privileges may be removed for a time.

Child signature: _____

Parent signature: _____

Date: _____

Device-Use Agreements at School

Device-use agreements aren't just a helpful tool for parents. Schools can use them as well. The Children's Internet Protection Act requires any school in the United States that accepts federal funding to help pay its internet bill—almost all do—to have an acceptable use policy (AUP) before it allows access to the school network.[17] This policy states what the school considers acceptable behavior for students using its network. Unfortunately, the vast majority of schools have totally missed the purpose of these agreements. They are often written like the fine print on a prescription medication advertisement. Just like creating home device agreements, the purpose of a school AUP shouldn't be legal protection; it should be about teaching kids to be effective digital citizens. Also, like home device agreements, the school should adapt the agreement to the student's level of understanding. A first-grader should not get the same device-use agreement as a junior in high school. You can check out the Renton school district in Washington and Champlain Valley school district in Vermont for good examples to model.[18] If you have kids in school, ask the principal if you can see the school's AUP. If it seems the school has lost the purpose of the document in legalese, suggest that the school check out the Consortium for School Networking's policy guide for rethinking AUPs.[19]

should. But we also need to be careful that our well-meaning attempts to help our kids don't depend on screen time as the sole determining factor of their digital regulation. By teaching the concept of digital balance, we help our children learn that all online activities are not created equal. Most importantly, we give them a framework to evaluate and adjust their own digital activities with far greater autonomy—one that will serve them throughout their entire lives.

Next Steps

Action Items

- As a family, turn off all unnecessary device/app notifications and autoplay features, and program necessary notifications to go silent during family times.

- Buy an alarm clock in order to prevent the need to sleep with devices nearby.

- Discuss bedtime and dinnertime tech breaks with your kids, and designate device-charging stations where devices live at night.

- With the help of your child, create a device-use agreement.

- Hold an app review and ask your kids to pitch their current apps to you. If an app is causing issues or doesn't seem to provide appropriate value, together come up with a deadline for when to remove that app and exchange it for a healthier alternative.

- Praise your child when you've noticed them self-regulating their device use particularly well.

Conversation Starters

- Have there ever been times when a particular app is keeping you from doing other things that are more important?

- What are some things that app developers do to make it harder for you to stop using their apps?

- How do you know when it's time to take a break from using technology?

- When are the times in our day that should be device free?

- How do you decide which apps should get more of your time than others?

4

Informed

Becoming Savvy Consumers of Information

When I was a kid, my mom bought me the *Encyclopedia Britannica*. It weighed 130 pounds (according, ironically, to Wikipedia). I remember being amazed at how much information I suddenly had access to, thanks to the entries in those books. At night, we would have "question time," when I would think of something I wanted to know more about and we'd try to find the answer in the pages of the encyclopedia. To me, this new access to information was empowering, but it also had limitations that as a kid, I didn't fully understand. The answers on the pages were frozen in time the moment they were printed. And the topics were limited to things that an editorial board sitting in Chicago decided were important enough to include, without knowing anything about my personal interests or goals.

Growing up today is entirely different. Through the internet, our children literally have access to all the world's information at their fingertips. There's no filter of editorial boards or outdated print versions to update. Initiatives like Project Gutenberg and Google Books give us searchable access to almost all the books in the entire world without having to leave our house. While my *Encyclopedia Britannica* provided around a hundred thousand explanations, Wikipedia provides over 6 million articles in English alone. Even the most obscure concepts appear with citations and links to deeper learning. Don't believe me? Go to Wikipedia and look up "spite house," "infinite monkey theorem," "towel day," "vampire numbers," or "The Great Molasses Flood." And thanks to millions of online DIY videos, our children can get someone to coach them through learning just about anything, from acing algebra to dancing the dubstep to building a bike. According to the World Economic Forum, the information contained on the internet is somewhere around 44 zettabytes. My entire *Encyclopedia Britannica* would have been about 1 gigabyte of information. To try to put that in perspective, a single zettabyte is the same as a trillion copies of the *Britannica*. If you were able to read my entire encyclopedia in one second, it would take you 31,700 years to read a single zettabyte of data. Times that by forty-four, and you have, roughly, the amount of information stored on the internet today. The floodgates are truly open.

Learning to Love Learning

Einstein famously said, "Information is not knowledge." Having access to all the information in the world doesn't seem to guarantee that we will actually use it. In our information-rich world, it is critical that we help our kids learn to love learning. Learning is the gateway to new discoveries, understanding others, and having a meaning to life. But most of all, learning brings a powerful sense of accomplishment. As kids learn, they feel more able to contribute to the world in a meaningful way, which is closely tied to their self-esteem. Years of social science research has shown that all our attempts to tell kids how special they are isn't nearly as effective at improving self-esteem as when they truly believe they have accomplished something noteworthy. Even an accomplishment as simple as correctly solving a math problem that was previously beyond their ability or learning to say a phrase in a new language can boost a child's confidence more than another gold star. This effect is even more pronounced when the thing they accomplish is valued by their family or community. When a child learns to fix a friend's broken bike, a team of kids win a debate competition, or a teenager helps a classmate translate something from English to Spanish, they feel a sense of purpose in what they're accomplishing. These positive reinforcements are powerful motivators for continued learning. Being an effective learner is also the foundation for the next three attributes of digital citizenship (that we will discuss in the coming chapters).

Developing a love of learning starts as simply as encouraging curiosity. We humans are deeply curious by nature. We all have things we want to know more about, even if it's something as trivial as what made that strange sound outside our window, or what Lady Gaga's real name is (it's Stefani Germanotta by the way). But the kind of curiosity we want to encourage is the proactive kind that chases after new information instead of waiting for something interesting to walk by. It's the kind of curiosity that doesn't come from external motivations (like grades, getting into college, bribes, or the threat of losing privileges). As powerful as those incentives may be at getting our kids to complete their assignments and make the honor roll, external motivations are much less effective at creating learners than a deep and genuine interest in the world. We all know from our own school experience that it is possible to optimize our efforts around getting an "A" without becoming the least bit interested in the topic. Curiosity, on the other hand, is the key to deeper learning. It leads to asking critical questions and engaging in complex reasoning. The good news is that, because humans are naturally curious, our job as parents isn't so much to create a love of learning as it is to encourage the interest in learning that's naturally there. Susan Engel, professor of psychology at Williams College and author of *The Hungry Mind: The Origins of Curiosity in Childhood*, offers several suggestions for encouraging curiosity in our children. Let me highlight two of them.

First, parents should show more interest in their kid's exploration than in their mastery. Curiosity is about gaining knowledge, not already having it. The pursuit of knowledge is a long and messy process, and our children quickly pick up on how we feel about it. If we enjoy learning, they will likely see it as fun. If we get frustrated or impatient with the learning process, they will likely feel that way as well. Engel makes the point that if we want to raise curious children, we need to show excitement when our kids express interest in learning to play the guitar, not just when they can play their first song. We need to look for the value in a science experiment that didn't go as planned, not just the one that won the science fair. Otherwise, children will devalue the process of learning, seeing it as nothing more than an annoying obstacle in the way of the end result.

The second suggestion from Engel is that parents need to create a family culture in which asking good questions is valued even more than having the right answers. In this kind of culture, family members are encouraged to wonder out loud. They often say things like, "I wonder why . . ." or "How might we . . ." They know that it's normal not to know everything and aren't bothered by not having all the answers. In this kind of home, parents also give their children the chance to work through tough questions on their own. It can take a lot of restraint not to give our kids the answer we know they're looking for, especially when we're busy, low on patience, or just tired. The more comfortable children are with their own limited understanding, the more comfortable they'll feel asking questions when they're in school, at work, and with friends, which, paradoxically, leads them to finding the answers faster than children who are obsessed with having the right answer. As a senior military officer once told me, "If you're not afraid to be wrong, you'll actually be right more often."

Modeling the Digital World as a Learning Tool

Encouraging curiosity with our kids changes the value proposition for their access to the digital world. With just a bit of modeling, curious learners begin to recognize the digital world as access to a super-powerful learning library, not just an entertainment machine. Modeling digital learning can happen at almost any moment. When a child finds a bug in the house, just asking a question like, "What type of bug do you think this is?" or "How many different types of bugs do you think there are in the world?" can turn it into a digital learning moment. It gives you a chance to model using digital access to find an answer to a question you clearly don't already know. By the way, I have actually done this and learned all kinds of fascinating things. For example, stink bugs are an invasive species in North America; they actually like the smell of their stink and communicate with each other using vibrations. Now, every time we come across a stink bug, that mundane experience has much more meaning.

Whenever the modeling can be tied to something that is relevant to a child's life, the better it is. When my son asks if that light in the sky at night is a star or a plane, it's the perfect opportunity to use an app like Sky Guide to help him find the answer. By pointing the phone at the sky, we might discover that the light is actually the planet Venus and that it is 162 million miles away. We might look up the circumference of the earth on Wikipedia (about 25,000 miles) and then calculate that 162 million miles is the same as going around the earth about 6,500 times. We could use the Wolfram Alpha app to get the speed of light (about 300,000 kilometers per second) and figure out it would take about 15 minutes for the light we're seeing to have traveled from Venus before it reaches our eyes.

You may be reading this and thinking, "If I took the time to look up every question my kid has in a day, I'd never get anything done!" Just as we don't need to offer new foods at every single meal in order to expand our children's palate, modeling our access to the digital world for learning isn't something you have to do every second of the day either. Even just an occasional modeling of answering questions using the digital tools is enough to help children see their technology devices as learning tools rather than only entertainment or communication tools. That's the goal.

Becoming Information Curators

Viewing the virtual world as a learning tool is one of the most powerful and necessary foundations for informed digital citizens. Elliott Masie, a renowned learning leader and innovator who coined the term "e-learning," says that in order to be successful in a zettabyte world, we must learn to become information curators. Curation is a term we usually associate with museums. Museum curation teams are responsible for collecting and storing artifacts and knowing how to pick the right artifacts from the collection to tell a story.

Several years ago, I had the opportunity to go into the basement of the Smithsonian National Museum of Natural History. Until then, I hadn't realized how much of the museum's collection was not on display. I was in a part of the paleobiology collection, which held a fraction of the nearly 150-million-piece total collection. The enormous room is filled with row after row of metal file cabinets, with aisles just wide enough to walk through. The drawers in the cabinets are shallower than traditional file cabinets, and each is filled with collections of bones from every imaginable animal. Hundreds of thousands of bones are neatly tagged and organized, some dating back millions of years.

Since there are costs to maintaining and preserving each item, the curators have the responsibility to select only pieces that have the most value to bring into the collection. Curators must also develop systems to store the artifacts in the collection. Not only does that mean making sure they are kept in a safe and dry space, but also that there is a system to tag and classify each item. After all, if you have 150 million artifacts but can't find the one you're looking for, the collection has very little value. The Smithsonian uses a process of tagging that assigns up to sixteen descriptions to each item, including the date added, type of animal, and the geolocation of the item in the museum's archives. When curators pull artifacts out of the collection to put on display, they need to know what items complement each other and align with the goals of the exhibit. Their goal is to tell a story through the right placement of pieces from the collection.

Making the Selection

Informed digital citizens need to learn how to become curators of information in the same way that museum curators make decisions about their collections. The first step in information curation starts with learning how to identify useful information out of zettabytes of junk. This is not a trivial skill. There are complicated eighteen-step processes for teaching kids to be effective finders of information online, but that's probably overkill. Here are three things we can do to model for our children to help them become effective digital curators:

1. *Ask good questions.* From a curation standpoint, a good question is one that most efficiently eliminates as much irrelevant information as possible and leads to the most-meaningful results. Most of the finding and selecting in the digital world starts with a search engine. When I was searching with my son to learn more about the brown marmorated stink bug, I explained that a good question might be "How many species of bugs are there in the world?" because if I searched for just "how many bugs," Google might have thought I was talking about the total number of bugs in the world (which is also an interesting, but different, question). Take a moment to show your children the advanced search options on Google (just search for "google advanced search" if you haven't been there before). You might show them how most search engines will

search for an exact phrase when words are put in quotations. This is particularly helpful when searching for a name or title. It's also important to reinforce that there is a wide variety of search tools. Take a minute to become familiar with a search engine other than Google, like DuckDuckGo, so they gain familiarity with multiple search tools. DuckDuckGo has the added benefit of not tracking or sharing your search history as other search engines do.

2. *Choose the best source.* After Google returns 72 million results in .44 seconds (jeez, do I have to wait all day?), we have the job choosing which results we will look at. For the stink bug example, I pointed out that there were answers from Quora, Smithsonian, and Wikipedia. We talked about which made the most sense for what we wanted to know. We could have talked about useful clues like whether the site has a .gov versus .com domain. However, the most important lesson for this step is modeling that the best information is not always the first result or even on the first page of results for any search. If the question relates to current events, sites like AllSides.com (which identifies bias in news reporting) might be particularly helpful for making the selection. If using a voice assistant for the search, pay attention to the source of the information provided and ask if it feels reliable.

3. *Evaluate the usefulness.* Once we select our digital information, we have to decide how much value it has for our purpose. This means evaluating the answer based on what we already know. We should get in the habit of asking, "Does that make sense given what else we've read?" Evaluating usefulness also means helping children become more comfortable with identifying the possible motives of the creator (is the goal to sell something, to persuade, to present research?). Digital media that are trying to sell something might be highly valuable if we're looking to make a purchase, but less so if we're looking for unbiased facts.

There are, of course, many other ways to find information beyond just doing a search. Signing up for daily news summaries or creating a custom Google Alert on a topic you care about will send you a message when new information is posted on the web. Subscribing to podcasts or video channels will do so as well. Elliott Masie points out that we should not forget about the power of using other people as part of our process for curating digital information. According to Masie, people who are really passionate about a topic tend to be great curators, because they'll go deep into the topic and will sort and select information with discernment. We can tap into them by following their digital presence or, if we know them personally, asking for their recommendations on related topics. A critical competency for successful digital citizens is knowing how to use their hive mind—the ability to tap into human experts when they need answers, not just search engines. (See "Tagging and Storing Information" for ideas to help organize digital content.)

Watch Out for Alternative Facts

Evaluating the usefulness of the information we find in the digital world is one of the most complex of any of the digital citizenship skills we will discuss in this book. Informed digital citizens must learn that all information does not have the same value. This is tricky to teach because it's a skill that adults aren't very good at either. The most obvious offender here is blatantly false information—fake news, as it has become known. Misinformation campaigns have existed since the dawn of time. In 1755, it was reported that the Lisbon earthquake was divine retribution against sinners. In 1835, the *New York Sun* became profitable reporting that there was an alien civilization on the moon.[1] But before mass adoption of digital tools, the spread and impact of misinformation was generally slow and limited. Now, in a world where the primary news source for two-thirds of Americans is Facebook, inaccurate information can be spread at an alarming rate.[2] With the underlying business model of social media platforms being advertising, there isn't really a business incentive to present information that

Tagging and Storing Information

Being able to find the right information at the right time is one of the most important competitive advantages in the digital world. In the early days of the internet, browser bookmarks were essentially the only way to tag and store digital content. Now there are a variety of strategies for tagging and storing digital media for future use. Here are some examples:

- **Playlists.** Tools like YouTube or Goodreads allow you to create collections of media by topic as well as subscribe to other people's playlist collections.

- **Albums.** Similar to playlists, tools like Google Photos allow collections of photos and videos with artificial intelligence built in to help identify people, without having to tag them manually.

- **Digital note-taking.** Tools like Simplenote, Evernote, or a variety of other personal note-taking tools can be powerful ways to capture and search notes and information that you've collected.

- **Tagged content.** Most social media sites allow you to tag or label content for easy retrieval. Pocket is a web app that lets you tag content from anywhere in the digital world in a single location.

- **Other people.** This last one may seem strange, but we can use other humans in our network to help with the task of curating digital media. By connecting to other people on sites like LinkedIn, we can take advantage of their curation abilities around particular topics.

is true, just information that will keep us scrolling and clicking. And this problem is not unique to Facebook. MIT researchers found that false information on Twitter is 70 percent more likely to be retweeted than the truth.[3] This has led to an explosion of misinformation. On

Election Day 2016, fake news actually outperformed real news in terms of number of views.[4]

We may be tempted to lower our filtering standards when friends and family share information with us, but we should be just as vigilant regardless of the source. A couple of years ago, in an attempt to reduce the spread of viral misinformation, Facebook experimented with changing its algorithms to make the news feed more focused on content from family and friends than on paid content. The hope was that this change would help stem the spread of fake news. The opposite happened. Prioritizing posts from family and friends actually increased the proliferation of misinformation, as people were less critical of inaccurate posts when shared by a family member. As a result, Facebook reverted to its original algorithm.[5] As parents, we need to model and teach fact-checking even when the source of information is a close friend or relative.

Perhaps the most vivid illustration of how little foundation children have in recognizing misinformation in a digital space comes from a landmark study published by Donald Leu, a researcher at the University of Connecticut.[6] Leu wanted to see how effective middle school children were at recognizing truth from fiction online. He created a simple but brilliant experiment. He worked with middle school teachers, who assigned students to research the most ridiculous thing he could possibly think of: an endangered Pacific Northwest tree octopus. There is, of course, no such thing as an endangered northwestern tree octopus, or any sort of cephalopod living in trees. Leu's study was simple. Count the number of students who recognized that the assignment was a total hoax, based on their ability to tell truth from fiction online.

The students went to the internet, where they found a website dedicated to preserving the northwest tree octopus, which Leu's team had created. The site was complete with descriptions of the habitat and feeding needs of the octopus and even a Photoshopped picture of an octopus climbing a snowy pine tree. What was the outcome? Only one student questioned the topic. All the rest finished the assignment, citing facts and details from the informative site they had found. These middle school students had been selected by their school as the top readers. How could they complete the assignment when everything they knew about pine forests and ocean life should have pointed to the absurdity? There was no other support for the idea on the internet than the one site manufactured by Leu's team.

Leu's study, while creative, had a relatively small sample size and only looked at students in the United States. Is it possible that a larger, more comprehensive study might show different results? Every three years, the Organisation for Economic Co-operation and Development administers the Programme for International Student Assessment, or PISA. The study is conducted in seventy-nine countries and measures fifteen-year-olds' ability to use their reading, mathematics, and science knowledge to meet real-life challenges. PISA is essentially the world's education report card. Whenever you hear statements comparing one country's education system to another—like "Finland has better schools than the United States" or "China is the best country in the world at teaching math"—the data for those statements comes from the PISA. For the first time, in 2018 PISA began measuring students' ability to recognize truth from fiction. Students were given opportunities to demonstrate their ability to choose facts that supported a claim. For example, they might be asked to make a case about the health benefits of chocolate by selecting the most appropriate resources to validate their conclusion. Nine in ten students worldwide were unable to successfully complete tasks that required them to determine the validity of information sources.[7]

Beyond Fake News

Not all manipulative digital media are blatantly fabricated. Digital citizens need to develop a "Spidey sense" for recognizing information that is manipulative by being used out of context, even if not technically false. A Stanford University study of eight thousand middle school, high school, and college students indicated a consistent failure in their ability to distinguish news from advertising, identifying the source of a tweeted fact, or recognizing that a website was created purely for marketing purposes.[8] It is particularly easy to get tripped up when looking at charts and graphs that have been manipulated to make a point. Data journalist Dan Kopf expressed frustration at how poorly we prepare young people to interpret visual representations of data. Kopf believes that there is a direct link between preserving our democracy and our children's ability to read charts.[9] "This isn't a trivial matter," says Kopf. "[A] lack of ability to interpret charts makes people more susceptible to being misled." As parents, we should be on the lookout for misleading charts or graphs to use as a learning opportunity for our children. They are easy to find all over the digital world.

Number of people on welfare

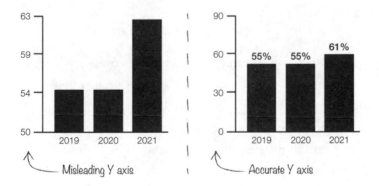

The two charts above show the same data about the number of people on welfare. But the one on the left has a manipulatively adjusted baseline on the Y axis to make it look like the number of people on welfare is spiking out of control. The same data is plotted at the right, but with the Y axis starting at 0, therefore showing only a slight change.

Covid infection rates

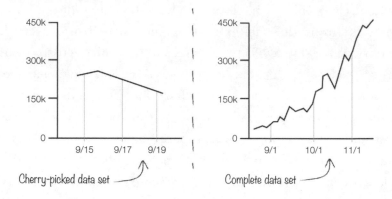

Cherry-picked data set

Complete data set

In this graphic, the chart on the left shows an example of cherry-picking a data range. By only showing a small section of the data, it appears as though the Covid-19 cases are going down, when in reality that is just a small dip in an overall very disturbing trend, as seen in the chart on the right, which shows the full data set.

Updating Our Tool Set

If being able to recognize reliable digital information is so important to our survival, why are we so bad at it? Are we just getting dumber the longer we spend time online? Hardly. With a huge amount of digital information passing in front of us on a given day, we are forced to make decisions about validity very quickly. The faster we can curate digital information, the more successful we are as members of the digital world. Because of this, we rely on a variety of shortcuts to help make quick judgments on the value of digital information. The problem is many of the shortcuts we use are borrowed from the physical world and don't serve us well in virtual spaces. As kids, many of us were taught if information was printed in a book, magazine, or newspaper, it was likely reliable. I remember learning the saying, "If it's in print, it has to be true." Print media were never free of errors or bias, but because printing was an expensive and cumbersome process, the

likelihood of having false information in print diminished. If someone invested the time and money to put something into print, they
had also likely done some fact-checking. Plus, they had to get someone to agree to distribute their book or magazine, which provided
another filter on the quality of print materials. So, if you had to make
a snap judgment, the fact that the information was in print wasn't an
unreasonable shortcut.

In the early 2000s, as the source of more of our information
migrated from the physical to the virtual world, the "print" shortcut
was no longer helpful. So, we evolved to find another shortcut: Does it
look like a credible source? In the early days of the internet, web design
was expensive and time-consuming. Building professional-looking
websites and graphics took complex code or the ability to design in
programs like Flash. It was fairly easy to tell a professional site from
someone's personal site based solely on the design and where it was
hosted (anyone remember Angelfire and GeoCities?). While also not
foolproof, the design of the site was a somewhat reliable shortcut to
the validity of its content. But now, with web platforms like Word-
Press or Squarespace, in just seconds anyone can download a theme
that looks more credible than the most prestigious university website.
Credible-sounding URLs can also be easily purchased for just a few
dollars. So once again, the shortcut of a credible-looking site no longer provides value.

So, what are some shortcuts we can teach our kids to rely on when
they need to quickly evaluate the value of digital media? We might
teach them to ask:

- Who is the author or creator? (Can you find anything else they
  have created?)

- Who is paying to make this content available? (Advertising revenue, a sponsoring organization, a paid subscription?)

- What is the goal of the author? (Share an opinion, present
  research, sell ads, and so on.)

- Is the content endorsed by an organization you trust?

- Do the URLs check out? (We read URLs from right to left, so media.**cnn**.com would be from CNN, but cnn.**media**.com would be from a site called media.com.)

- Can you validate the claims with another source? (Are there citations to support the claims of the material? If it sounds like a stretch, does a search on a fact-checking site like Snopes reveal anything?)

- How old is the information?

- Does the content use hyperbolic, alarmist, or emotional language?

- Do photos or graphs appear manipulated? (Use Google Image search or TinEye.com to see where else the images have been used; check for tricks on graph presentation.)

These questions can be answered in less than a minute and can quickly tease out whether a source of digital media is appropriate for our intended purpose. There are also some great tools that can help us. Sites like PolitiFact, FactCheck.org, and Snopes do a great job of fact-checking news.

New Forms of Learning

As we wrap up this chapter on creating informed digital citizens, we should recognize that the digital world has done more for learning than just put a massive pile of information at our fingertips. It has also enabled new modes of learning that simply weren't possible in the physical world. These new approaches can help us overcome some of the limitations inherent to learning in a classroom. When the coronavirus pandemic forced nearly a billion children to stay home, there

Should We Trust Wikipedia?

Curating information can be done individually, but it can also be done as a group activity. Group curation can be particularly helpful when dealing with large amounts of information that would be overwhelming for any one person to make sense of on their own. One of the most successful examples of group curation can be seen in the Wikipedia community. While everyone has heard of Wikipedia, its purpose continues to be misunderstood. I cringe when I hear parents or teachers advising against using Wikipedia because it's not a reliable source of information. That's like saying, "Don't go to the symphony because one of the violists might play a wrong note." But it also exposes a deeper lack of understanding of the key role Wikipedia plays in curating our digital world. Let's set the record straight.

First, Wikipedia has *never claimed* to be a reliable source (its own "about" page states, "Wikipedia does not consider itself to be a reliable source"). A whole series of studies have been conducted over the years to show the accuracy of Wikipedia articles, some showing highly accurate results, others pointing out glaring errors.[10] Even with the errors, Wikipedia is still likely more accurate than much of the content in your child's textbooks. But the real question is what value does Wikipedia bring if it's not a reliable source?

It turns out Wikipedia isn't trying to solve a reliability problem; it's trying to solve a curation problem. In the digital world, trying to find reliable answers in the deluge of digital noise is nearly impossible if you don't already have some baseline information about a topic. It's what I call the "you don't know what you don't know" problem. One of the most challenging catch-22s in your child's learning journey in the digital world is that without already knowing key terms, people, or concepts about a topic, it can be easy to be misled. If I know nothing about black holes, I don't even have the basic information I need to start to learn about them. *This* is the problem Wikipedia solves. A quick trip

(continued)

to the Wikipedia page about black holes would introduce me to concepts such "general relativity" and "event horizon" or people like Karl Schwarzschild and John Michell. It equips me to begin a more informed learning journey. Wikipedia even gives me the next step by providing a list of sources that *are* reliable at the bottom of each page. The article on black holes offers two hundred of them. Wikipedia is the best jumping-off point for learning the world has ever had. There is even a Simple English version of Wikipedia to help younger readers. So instead of teaching our kids to avoid Wikipedia, we should be encouraging them to use it as the best starting point for deeper learning journeys.

---

was a mass migration to online learning experiences. The rushed move to online learning exposed some of its rough edges to be sure, but it also exposed some of the long-standing inequities of face-to-face learning that could be solved in the digital world. Here are three examples.

Accessing Expertise

Education in the physical world requires teachers and students to live and learn in close physical proximity. This creates particular challenges for students in regions where an experienced teacher for a particular subject may simply not be available. When I worked in the US Senate, I visited with education leaders from Omak, Washington, a town with a total population of less than five thousand. The superintendent of Omak schools shared that he had been trying unsuccessfully to fill a math teacher position for five years. There simply weren't enough qualified math teachers living near Omak, not to mention computer science, physics, or orchestra teachers. This is true for hundreds of thousands of schools around the world. Yet learning in the virtual world is ambivalent to the physical location of the participants. Access to expertise becomes possible for all students, regardless of where they live.

This doesn't just mean access to other classroom teachers but experts of all types. I recently observed a class at Los Angeles Unified School District where children from an elementary school had the opportunity to use videoconferencing tools to interview elected leaders about their position on environmental issues. When Stacey Moore's third-grade class at Three Oaks Elementary School in Virginia Beach was learning about animals in Africa, instead of just showing pictures, they decided to go on a virtual safari. Moore arranged for a safari guide to strap on a GoPro camera and take the kids on a live safari experience from their classroom. The students observed the animals in their natural habitats as they asked questions of the wildlife expert along the way.

Addressing Accessibility

Learning in the physical world can be challenging for kids with unique needs. Technology brings a variety of supports to make learning accessible to all learners. Kids who have trouble seeing can use technology to increase font sizes or have a text read or interpreted for them. A young person learning another language can leverage translation tools to better understand the learning materials. A whole host of technologies are available to help students overcome physical challenges that could otherwise limit learning.

I met Kyle Weintraub when he was a seventh-grade student at David Posnack School in Davie, Florida. He had been diagnosed with lymphoma and had to travel from his hometown to Philadelphia to receive lifesaving treatment. Weintraub's school bought a robot that he could control remotely from his hospital room in Philadelphia. Through the robot, Weintraub was able to participate in his classes, maintain friendships, and ask questions, all without leaving his hospital room.

As parents, we should be aware of the wide range of digital supports that are available to help children who experience physical, emotional, or cognitive challenges to learning and advocate for their appropriate use. Working with your school or visiting sites like CAST. org can provide additional insights into the tools and approaches that technology brings to lower the barriers to learning for students with unique needs.

Personalizing Learning

One of the most significant limitations of learning in the physical world is that it is difficult and expensive to adapt learning experiences to the needs of individual learners. All children have different interests and talents, different backgrounds and goals. Yet we continue to group kids by age into batches of twenty to thirty as if school was a factory. Todd Rose, an education researcher at Harvard University, is challenging our traditional views of learning progress. His research focuses on the idea that learning is jagged.[11] In other words, everyone has areas in which they have more expertise than others and areas where they have less. People can be experts in one area, even while they are complete novices in another, and there isn't a consistent order to what skills they gain before others. This jagged pattern of expertise and inexperience is unique to every single learner.

While learning in the physical world has little ability to accommodate our jagged learning needs, digital tools can do a much better job of adapting to our unique interests and skill levels. At a very basic level, this can mean allowing kids to progress based on their ability to demonstrate understanding, not based on a rigid class syllabus. A variety of digital tools can help identify which concepts our children may be struggling with and provide individualized recommendations to students, teachers, and parents tailored to their needs. Effective personalized learning does not mean having all instruction presented by computer. But true personalized learning leverages technology to provide real-time feedback on student progress and to help parents and teachers customize learning pace and activities to align to each child's needs and interests. (To learn more about using technology to transform learning, visit www.ISTE.org.)

Futurist Alvin Toffler once said, "The illiterate of the twenty-first century will not be those who cannot read and write, but those who cannot learn, unlearn, and relearn." Informed digital citizens recognize the importance of being lifelong learners. They know how to recognize true and false information. They know how to find meaningful content in a crescendo of digital noise. They experience new learning models made possible by the digital tools. But above all, they view their access to the digital world as a passport to the most powerful learning library ever known. As parents, it's our job to encourage children's natural curiosity and enable them to find trusted sources of digital information on their path to lifelong learning.

Next Steps

Action Items

- When your child shows interest in a subject (a sport, nature, a song, an event in history, and so on), find an app, video, or website that helps them explore the topic in greater depth.

- Look for opportunities to praise your child for the effort they've put into learning a task that they haven't yet mastered, rather than focusing solely on results.

- Look for examples of misleading or blatantly false digital media and talk with your kids about some shortcuts that could be used to identify it as such.

- Try using a tool like Padlet or Wakelet to create custom collections of media to share with your kids.

- Explore Advanced Google Search or DuckDuckGo to see what different search options are available.

- Create a Google Alert with your kids for something they care about.

Conversation Starters

- How do you know when something you see online is believable?

- Why do you think people are willing to believe things a family member shares with them online even if they're not true?

- What are the dangers of not recognizing when something we see online is misleading?

- What should you do if you share something and then you find out that it wasn't true?

- How might you respond when someone you know shares or posts information that appears to be incorrect?

- What are your favorite places to go online when you want to learn something new?

- What is something new that you've learned online recently?

5

Inclusive

Balancing Multiple Viewpoints with Respect

One of the great benefits of growing up in the digital world is that our children have many more opportunities to engage with diverse ideas and viewpoints on any given topic. They can learn and develop a deeper understanding of issues more quickly than we ever did as kids. But their ideas and beliefs will be challenged frequently, unlike our experience growing up in an unplugged world. If we don't prepare young people to understand how to value and respect multiple, opposing viewpoints, they may forfeit one of their greatest learning opportunities and, worse, treat people who hold opposing viewpoints disrespectfully. In this chapter, we will explore some strategies for teaching our kids to respect multiple viewpoints and create a more inclusive virtual world for themselves and others.

Understanding How Our Brains Work

One of the first steps in helping our kids learn to be inclusive in virtual spaces is helping them understand the cognitive processes that cause people to belittle someone else's viewpoint or treat them disrespectfully. I'll illustrate this with a personal example. For years, we had a rule in our house that we couldn't eat sugary cereals for breakfast. We banned Froot Loops and Frosted Flakes and encouraged healthy cereals like Raisin Bran and Cheerios. Every time I stuck to my guns during a grocery-aisle tantrum over Fruity Pebbles, I felt like a good parent. One day, after giving my wife a hard time for buying a box of Lucky Charms, I happened to look at the nutritional information on the box as it sat next to my granola. To my complete disbelief, the sugar content on both boxes was identical.

Psychology researchers call the moment when we are presented with information that challenges our existing understanding "cognitive dissonance." These moments are necessary for us to learn and grow, but they are also uncomfortable. In fact, our brains are evolutionarily wired to avoid them because reevaluating our existing beliefs takes a lot of brain power. It's less work for us to be right than wrong. As such, our brain prioritizes making us *feel* correct over figuring out whether or not we actually *are* correct.[1] As the graphic on the next page shows, this can cause us to grab on to hunches that align with our existing beliefs over facts that don't in order to avoid the energy-consuming reevaluation process. This is formally known as certainty bias.[2] When we experience cognitive dissonance, our brains first look for a way to reject the conflicting information.

As I stared at the nutritional information on the side of the cereal box, the easiest way forward, cognitively speaking, would have been to reject the new information. I might have told myself that the nutritional facts were incorrect or the process for measuring sugar in cereals was flawed. By doing so, my old way of thinking about cereal could have remained intact with little energy required from my brain. I could have continued my prohibition on sugary cereals and avoided having

How we react to new data

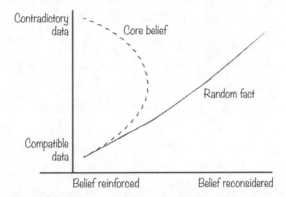

to tell my wife that I was wrong. On the other hand, if I had chosen to accept the new information, I would have had to admit that my previously held belief about cereal was incorrect—that Frosted Flakes were in fact no more sugary than Raisin Bran. Fortunately, in most circumstances, there is a third path to resolving cognitive dissonance—one that is critically important for us to teach young people if they are to be inclusive members of our digital world. The third path is to develop a more nuanced understanding of the situation that allows us to simultaneously hold on to truth from multiple sources. This is how we gain a deeper understanding of the world around us.

In the case of the cereals, I might have come to understand that sugar is only one indicator of nutritional value. Raisin Bran has much more fiber and whole grain than Frosted Flakes, which means that it is still a healthier choice, even though both are loaded with sugar. Or I might have realized that eating less sugary cereals is still a solid health principle, but that the names of the cereals are not a good indicator of how much sugar they contain. Either way, I would have deepened my understanding because I was able to recognize value from multiple sources of information. This may not sound so hard when we're talking about cereal, but if the new information challenges one of our core beliefs (who our heroes are, our gender or cultural identity, our national allegiance, and so on), it can be very hard to find the value of an opposing view. The impulse to defend a core belief is so powerful that it can take a huge amount of effort to keep from discrediting and devaluing the source of the information without any consideration. This defense mechanism sidesteps cognitive dissonance, taking away opportunities to learn and, if we're not careful, can make us less tolerant of those with differing beliefs.

Simply recognizing what is happening and talking about these reactions with our kids can make a huge difference in their ability to be respectful people in virtual spaces. We might look for opportunities to talk with our kids about how they feel when they encounter a viewpoint online that contradicts their own. We can help them understand that seeing value in an alternative viewpoint does not mean having to give up their own viewpoint. We can practice by finding differing viewpoints on a given topic in the news online and discuss what we can learn from each. Another activity might be to call out examples of digital media that have been intentionally designed to make us feel *more* cognitive dissonance, like making an opposing political view seem even more extreme than it is. By so doing, we recognize a divisive strategy to make opposing viewpoints seem more foreign than they actually are in order to make them easier to reject.

For older kids, an interesting way to help them understand the additional cognitive effort required to value differing viewpoints is to have them take Harvard's implicit bias test (available online).[3] The test is very simple. After entering some basic demographic information about yourself, you answer questions on several topics for which you have inherent bias. Let's say you are a heterosexual male and choose the sexual orientation bias test. You would see a series of words and icons on the screen and would be asked to sort them as either good or bad. For the first round, words or icons related to homosexuality would be sorted as bad, and words or icons related to being heterosexual would be sorted as good. In the next round, you would see the same items, but this time you would be tasked with labeling all of the words related to homosexuality as good and all of the items related to heterosexuality as bad. The test measures how much longer it takes you, as a heterosexual male, to make the sorting decisions when your inherent bias is associated with good versus bad. The results are surprising to almost everyone who takes the test. Even after taking it several times, I always score lower in labeling something as good if it runs counter to my own demographic. It doesn't mean that I am homophobic; it just reveals that our brains have to exert more effort to process ideas that differ from our default position.

Increasing our children's awareness that their natural instincts are working against them when it comes to processing viewpoints that are different from their own can help them become more inclusive digital citizens. This awareness can help them model and increase tolerance and value the varied perspectives shared in our virtual world.

Seeing the Person behind the Belief

A second key strategy for creating inclusive and tolerant digital citizens is to help them recognize that there are real people behind the ideas they encounter online. While the virtual world allows us to engage with more viewpoints, it also allows us to detach a viewpoint from the person generating it. Teaching inclusivity means addressing a double-whammy effect of the nature of our online interactions. The first whammy is that we are shielded from the effects of intolerance online, as we generally do not see the impact of our actions in the same way we would in the physical world.

Shortly after I got my license as a teenager, I was driving home from school. I got to a four-way stop sign and waited my turn to proceed. When it was my turn, a car from the other side of the intersection pulled ahead (out of turn), causing me to have to swerve quickly to avoid an accident. In an act of teenage intolerance, I made a particular hand gesture to communicate my anger. What happened next is something I will never forget. I saw the driver, not the reckless kid I had imagined, but an older man who could have been my grandfather. He had a look of embarrassment on his face because of the mistake he knew he had made. As we passed, he held up his hands and mouthed the words "I'm so sorry." The impact of seeing his embarrassment juxtaposed with my unkind response was more than I could take. I pulled over to the side of the road and cried. I decided that I would never again use my fingers to respond to someone who was not driving well.

But imagine if I hadn't ever seen the person in that car or known what his reaction had been. I would never have received the feedback of how inappropriate my response was to his honest mistake. My mental narrative would have led me to believe it was the deliberate act of an irresponsible teenager—none of which was true. Virtual spaces allow us to avoid seeing the results of our actions. A hurtful comment made in the virtual world may be just as wounding as in the physical world, but we don't witness the damage in the same way. When we can't see the impact of our digital actions, our empathy decreases. When we are spared from having to deal with the consequences of the things we do and say online, we can easily treat other people poorly without even intending to do so. I've often wondered how inclusivity in virtual spaces would change if every time we made a post about someone else on social media, the platform would first show us a preview of that same post as if someone were making it about *us*. In the absence of such a feature, as parents we must teach our children to develop that skill for themselves. We might ask how they would feel if a post or comment they made was instead written about them by someone else.

Talking to People Who Hate Me

Writer and activist Dylan Marron is the creator of a widely followed YouTube channel dedicated to addressing tough social issues—the kinds of issues that hit right at our core beliefs. He also focuses on helping teach inclusivity in online spaces. His YouTube series "Unboxing" mimics the popular videos in which people unpack material items they've purchased to show others what comes in the box. But instead of unboxing a PlayStation or an Instant Pot, Marron metaphorically unpacks tough social issues like white privilege or Islamophobia. Not surprisingly, his videos attract a lot of responses; many are harshly critical of his viewpoints.

Marron told me he used to respond to his detractors by hitting back, making fun of their comments, and so on. But one day, Marron decided to look at the social media pages of his commenters in order to better understand the human behind the vitriol and maybe find a way to give them the benefit of the doubt. This is where the story gets interesting. Marron chose to reach out to some of these criticizers to see if they'd be willing to talk with him by phone. Several of them agreed. (I should point out here that Marron contacted people who were harshly critical but did not appear to present any danger to him.)

During these conversations, Marron learned some important lessons. One was that if you want to create positive change, you have to speak *with* people who disagree with you, not *at* them. He also learned that having a meaningful conversation required him first to find a way to empathize with the person on the phone and maybe gain some empathy in return. Marron said that offering empathy is a generous and vulnerable act to make toward someone who has publicly belittled you or your ideas. Empathizing with people with opposing viewpoints doesn't justify disrespectful comments or assume that either person's viewpoint will change. Marron shared, "Empathizing with someone you profoundly disagree with does not suddenly compromise your own deeply held beliefs and endorse theirs. It just means that I'm acknowledging the humanity of someone who was raised to think very differently from me." (You can hear some recordings of his conversations on the *Conversations with People Who Hate Me* podcast.)

As parents, we don't have to set up calls with people who disagree with us online to teach our kids how to be tolerant and kind in virtual spaces. But we do have to practice empathy in our families and model the appropriate behavior when we come across posts or digital media that contradict our own views. One way to do this is to practice explaining an issue from someone else's point of view. We don't have to agree with them to learn to understand another person's viewpoint: "While we believe [insert viewpoint here], you can see how someone who had experience of [insert experience here] might feel very differently about this issue." Alternatively, we can open up the discussion for debate. Ask two members of your family to represent each side of a viewpoint, without allowing name-calling or saying the other is wrong. This can help them think through the opposing position before rushing to judgment.

Diversify Our Digital Diet

The second whammy that we must address in order to teach inclusivity is recognizing that our virtual third places have been designed to reinforce our existing viewpoints. Think back to our conversation about cognitive dissonance. Ideas that challenge previously held notions are stressful. Most virtual shared spaces are funded by ad revenue, meaning the platform providers make money by keeping our eyes on their site (and their ads) for as long as possible. In order to do so, they need to keep us comfortable so we will keep scrolling and clicking. Thus, the platforms we use in the virtual world have been systematically designed to limit cognitive dissonance.

In chapter 1, we met computer programmer-turned-sociologist Zeynep Tufekci, who studies the design of social media algorithms. She tells us that the algorithms built into virtual community spaces can easily infer things about us and our family members, including ethnicity, religion, personality traits, intelligence, happiness, use of addictive substances, and parental separation, just based on the things we click on and "like." The algorithms may also be able to detect age, gender, and even sexual orientation from our profile pictures. Armed with that information, the platforms can then present as few opposing beliefs as possible so we feel more comfortable continuing to spend time there—this is called the "bubble effect." And it works with stunning accuracy. Because our social media feeds reinforce our beliefs, we actually begin to feel as if everyone else in the world believes the same way we do. While this reduces cognitive dissonance, if unchecked, it can also make us feel artificially "in the right" all the time.

Tufekci also found that algorithms don't just show us more of our same beliefs, but more-extreme versions of those beliefs. The next video recommendation will be more extreme than the last. She observed that after watching several videos of a Donald Trump rally, for instance, the subsequent videos were not just more Trump rallies, but more-extreme messages centered around white supremacy. And Tufekci is quick to point out that this is not unique to any one ideology; it's a design that takes any view on any topic and brings it to the extreme. Tufekci says, "I experimented with nonpolitical topics. The same basic pattern emerged. Videos about vegetarianism led to videos about veganism. Videos about jogging led to videos about running ultramarathons. It seems as if you are never 'hard core' enough for YouTube's recommendation algorithm."[4]

In a perfect world, we could control the level of echo provided by our shared virtual spaces through personalized settings. We could choose whether we want only content that reinforces our existing opinions, content that only shows us opposing viewpoints, or a balance somewhere in between. Since it's unlikely that we will ever have such an option, teaching our kids to be aware of the bubble effect can have a major impact on counteracting it. We can encourage and model the practice of seeking news from a variety of sources that represent a range of viewpoints on a particular issue to counteract the dangerous perception of feeling perpetually in the right.

Focusing on Others Online

When Sanah Jivani was twelve years old, she experienced an unexpected change in her life. One morning, she woke up to find all of her hair lying on her pillow. It had completely fallen out overnight. Later, Jivani learned that she had a hair loss condition called alopecia. I had a chance to talk with Jivani at a Digital Citizenship event in

California. She says it's hard to find words to describe how devastating her experience was for a girl in middle school. "I immediately bought a wig to cover up my insecurity and hurt," she recalls. The kids at her school were far from supportive—guessing all of the reasons why she was now wearing a wig. She was mortified by comments such as "maybe she's doing it all so people will finally like her" or "she probably just wants attention."[5]

Yet, despite her peers' hurtful comments, Jivani decided to make a bold move. One day, she removed her wig and shared a video online showing the world that she wasn't ashamed to be herself. Jivani now considers that to be one of the best days of her life, as she recalls something unexpected that happened. After sharing the video, other kids from around the world saw her brave act and began to open up about their own personal challenges. "We created an online community of hope and support," recalls Jivani. "Hearing their stories changed my life, and I knew I had to keep sharing my story. I was proud to be myself and felt supported by an amazing digital community." Jivani says that every young person deserves to be part of an online community of supporters who make them feel safe and included—one that encourages them to be their full selves.

Our well-intentioned attempts to address online dangers have generally focused on protecting the potential victim. Every parent worries about their kid being bullied online. So we teach our kids how to keep themselves safe, but often skip the actions they can take to create a safe environment for others. This approach is, frankly, a bit selfish. Being inclusive online requires taking actions to make sure others feel safe and respected in virtual spaces as well. All the responsibility should not be on the potential victim to stop intolerance. Alert digital citizens know how to switch from being bystanders to upstanders.

In Pittsburgh, a group of kids started a movement with the specific purpose of teaching this lesson. Julia and Amelia, students at the Avonworth Primary Center, approached their teacher with an idea to start a campaign to encourage their peers to be kinder to others. They decided to make shirts with the simple message, "Be The Kind Kid." With a team of students, Julia and Amelia have now distributed over fifty thousand shirts spreading their simple but powerful message. Being the kind kid online means being quick to invite and include someone who may be left out of a virtual space.

Taking Lessons from the Physical World

As we think about teaching our kids to be inclusive online, perhaps we can draw inspiration from teaching inclusivity in the physical world. It's true, we have a long way to go when it comes to being tolerant and inclusive in the physical world, as Jivani's experience shows. There are still far too many examples where exclusion and intolerance go unchecked, for both kids and adults. Yet even with many gaps to close, teaching tolerance in the physical world has at least become baked into the process of growing up. If you are the parent of more than one child, teaching this concept likely consumes a large portion of your parenting life. Learning not to exclude a brother or fight with a sister is one of the first life lessons that we teach. Kindergarten teachers are masterful at this; the classroom is often one of the first places where children participate in a shared physical space outside their family. Kindergarten teachers are adept at turning every "he-stole-the-blue-crayon-from-me-so-I-punched-him" moment into a learning opportunity. "Hitting your classmate is not how we solve problems. Let's practice asking if we can take a turn . . ." They read stories like Dr. Seuss's *The Sneetches* and describe how everyone loses when we exclude people. Yes, there is a reason for those "All I really need to know I learned in kindergarten" posters.

As children get older, other activities kick in. We read books like *To Kill a Mockingbird* or *The Sun Is Also a Star* in English class. Many schools offer Model Legislature or debate clubs, designed specifically to teach young people how to disagree with another person's position without making personal attacks. In a debate club, there is a good chance you won't even agree with the position you've been asked to take. Earlier in this book, we talked about the concept of sign-posting (reminding people of good social behaviors through messages posted in public places). We sign-post around inclusivity in physical spaces all the time. Schools have signs that remind people "Everyone Is Welcome Here" or "Be a Hero: Be Kind." Perhaps these activities can give us ideas for developing systemic approaches for practicing inclusivity in the virtual world as well.

Practicing Inclusivity in Virtual Spaces

As we try to bring the same level of attention to modeling inclusive practices into our digital world, we should start by making sure our kids are actively practicing being good cyberfriends, including talking through how they might respond in situations when someone else is being treated unkindly in a virtual space. Even if our kids are not committing acts of intolerance themselves, if they are witnessing acts of intolerance and choose to do nothing, they are complicit. We might think that in an online environment with many more people available to intervene, someone would more likely stand up for a person who is being treated unfairly. Unfortunately, the opposite is true. The virtual world is particularly prone to the bystander effect, which occurs when multiple people observe a problem and nobody takes action because they all assume someone else will. In a self-fulfilling prophecy, when it appears that nobody is acting, we assume that it must be appropriate not to act as well. Ninety-five percent of teens who have witnessed cruel behavior on social networking sites say they also have witnessed others ignoring the behavior.[6] We can challenge our kids to look for opportunities to stand up for someone who is being treated unkindly online and celebrate them when they have the courage to do so.

As parents, we should openly share examples when we've advocated for someone ourselves. We can also share examples of how we respectfully offered differing viewpoints to opinions shared online. And we should point out when we see political leaders or celebrities using their digital media presence in a disrespectful way, regardless of whether or not we agree with their position. According to Sanah Jivani, it is imperative that, as families, we actively talk about how we can create inclusive and accepting online communities.

Hate Is Contagious—but So Is Kindness

We hear so many examples of the escalating divisiveness and anger that exist in virtual spaces. It feels as if animosity is contagious. But the good news is that kindness is contagious, too. I'm often surprised by how little effort it takes to turn unkindness around, even in virtual spaces where the more nuanced forms of communication, such as tone of voice and body language, are missing. Most acts of intolerance stop as soon as a bystander intervenes on behalf of someone who is being disrespected.[7] When Kristen Layne wanted to buy a new prom dress, she decided to get the money she needed by selling her old prom dress online. She posted a picture of herself wearing the dress to GoFundMe for people to bid on. Unfortunately, some of the responses were cruel, pointing out her weight and making fun of her appearance. With great restraint, she responded by bravely saying, "Can you please stop with the comments? Sorry that I'm not pleasing to your eye." But unfortunately the taunting didn't stop; it got worse. If I stopped the story here, you might guess how it would end, perhaps with yet another case of someone getting bullied to the point of taking their own life.

Only it didn't. Not long after the hateful comments began, one person decided to move from being a bystander to an upstander, actively creating a more inclusive virtual world by posting that she thought Layne looked "stunning" and "beautiful on the inside and out." Others then followed and began flooding the comments section with uplifting messages of encouragement. Layne said the uplifting comments made her feel better about herself and realize she was not alone. In what became a community effort to stand up to digital intolerance, hundreds of people began flooding Layne's page with kind comments. She ended up receiving over $5,000 in donations to buy her new dress, much of which she used to help other students who weren't able to afford their own dresses.[8]

By moving from being bystanders to active advocates, our children can become ambassadors for a more inclusive digital world. While our physical world is still largely segregated based on where we live, our digital world brings an opportunity for cross-pollination of urban and suburban, poor and wealthy, east and west, sick and well, vegan and cattle rancher, millennial and boomer, socialist and libertarian, Yankees fan and Red Sox fan. These diverse connections exponentially increase the number of times our brains confront ideas that challenge our existing views. If we quickly reject new ideas—and the people who present them—we are reinforcing our certainty bias. Yet when we can become comfortable with and try to understand a differing viewpoint, we are in a position to do some of our most important learning.

We aren't teaching our children to include others only because it's a nice thing to do. We are teaching them that their knowledge is limited and that one of the best ways they can fill the gaps in their understanding is by learning from others whose experiences and perspectives differ from their own. As a result, our tiny corner of the internet can becomes a place where people with differing ideologies can be respected and included.

Next Steps

Action Items

- Learn more about how our brains react to new information (consider reading *What Makes Your Brain Happy and Why You Should Do the Opposite* by David DiSalvo), and share your learning with your children.

- Follow a group on Facebook, Instagram, or other social platform that promotes civil but contrasting beliefs from yours, or sign up for an e-newsletter from a trusted news organization that supports views different from your own.

- If you have older kids, take the Harvard implicit bias test together and discuss the results.

- Invite a friend who has an opposing viewpoint to explain their position to you. Listen and ask clarifying questions without debating. Talk with your children about your experience and encourage them to find a similar opportunity to listen.

- Look for examples of bias or assumptions online (they're everywhere) and point them out to your kids.

- Practice having different members of your family respectfully debate different sides of an issue.

Conversation Starters

- Why is it important to hear viewpoints from people who think differently than you?

- What would happen if nobody ever challenged your beliefs?

- Can you think of something you've learned from someone who disagreed with you?

- Have you ever regretted something you've written or said online?

- Have you ever seen someone you respect do or say something online that disappointed you?

- Why do you think it's easier to be unkind to someone online than in person?

- Have you ever felt excluded or rejected online?

- How can you make sure others feel included in your online groups?

- What should you do if you're participating in an online group where someone is being made fun of or picked on?

6

Engaged

Using Tech to Make Our Communities Better

In the book *The Spyglass*, children's author Richard Paul Evans describes a kingdom that has fallen into disrepair and apathy.[1] Crops were planted and then failed, houses were built and then neglected, people were impoverished and dispirited. One day a traveler arrives at the crumbling palace to meet with the king. The traveler explains that he has an enchanted spyglass. Anyone who looks through the spyglass is able to see things not as they are but as they could be. With the help of the enchanted spyglass, the king begins to see potential in every part of his dilapidated kingdom in ways he never had imagined before. Ignited by this new hope, the king inspires his subjects to work alongside him to build a beautiful land, because he knows what the kingdom has the potential to become. As the book ends, the reader sees that the kingdom is repaired and thriving; it has become the vision shown by the spyglass.

Engaged digital citizens view technology like the spyglass; it is a tool that we can use to help make the communities we live in—both digital and physical—reach a higher potential. In chapter 3, we learned about the difference between active and passive tech use. Passive tech users see technology as a tool to consume information and entertain themselves, whereas active tech users view technology, like the spyglass, as a tool to help improve the world around them. The simple mindset shift in viewing our devices as tools for doing good is the defining characteristic of engaged digital citizens.

Young Voices Matter

The first step for creating engaged digital citizens is making sure we're teaching young people that their contributions and opinions matter. I think deep down we all believe this and want it to be true. But there are many elements of our society that are set up to communicate the opposite message. Much of school is designed in a way that tells our kids that they are to apply the skills they are learning some day in their hypothetical future, not now. They are taught to learn math because they will need it to get into college. They are taught to write because it will be an important skill when they get a job. In history, the people they learn about are always adults, not kids. They have little choice or control over the learning experience itself; they are handed a schedule, given assignments (that they didn't have any input in designing), and told to complete them by a date that they didn't choose. The message that young voices don't matter is reinforced by the fact that they can't vote until they are eighteen. One of the most important tenets of democracy is the idea that everyone has a voice. We teach that to our children, yet we offer very few ways to actually *use* that voice before they're no longer kids. Fortunately, the digital world gives a wide set of tools that can help change that narrative. These tools allow youth to have a voice and learn how to make a meaningful impact on their community, family, and in some cases, the world as a whole—right now, not decades down the road.

Just Some Students from Florida

In February 2018, Marjory Stoneman Douglas High School in Parkland, Florida, was in the news worldwide when nineteen-year-old Nikolas Cruz entered the school with a semiautomatic rifle, killing seventeen people and injuring seventeen others. This horrific event became one of the deadliest school shootings in US history. Yet there was a unique ending to this tragic story that set it apart for another reason. In other school shootings, traditional news media and political leaders quickly shape the national conversation around the event. A narrative emerges around what actually happened, with speculation about the causes, who is to blame, and the political responses to justify action (or lack thereof). But in the case of Parkland, it was the students who shaped the national conversation. Frustrated about viewpoints and conclusions from adults that they did not share or agree with, they used their access to social media to reset and redirect the conversation into what has now become one of the most powerful examples of youth engagement ever seen. Within a week of the shooting, the students had appeared on nearly every major news program and had raised more than $3 million in donations to support their cause. Emma Gonzáles, one of the most recognizable faces of the movement, has over 1.5 million Twitter followers—about twice as many as the National Rifle Association.[2]

Not long after the shooting, I met Diane Wolk-Rogers, a history teacher at Marjory Stoneman Douglas. As she explained, nobody could have prepared these students for the horror they faced on that day. But they had been prepared to know how to use technology to make their voices heard. Wolk-Rogers says, "They are armed with incredible communication skills and a sense of citizenship that I find so inspiring." So when it was time to act, they knew the tools of the trade.

Engaged digital citizens know how to use technology to identify and propose solutions and promote action around causes that are important to them and their communities.[3] Micro-activism is a term used to describe small-scale efforts that, when combined, can bring about significant change. While young people might not be able to vote or run for office, they have a whole range of micro-activism opportunities—all made possible by their participation in the digital world. For youth who have access to social media, micro-activism can be as simple as using their digital platforms to call awareness to issues that matter to them—eradicating racism, protecting our planet, or funding their school, and so on. Most states have a function on their website to submit ideas or feedback directly to the office of the governor. Through sites like Change.org anyone, regardless of age, can submit suggestions to political leaders or private sector entities. You can also add your name in support of other petitions that are gaining momentum. There are many compelling stories of youth who have used Change.org to call attention to issues that matter to them. Examples include a ten-year-old who used the platform to convince Jamba Juice to switch from Styrofoam cups to a more environmentally friendly alternative. Or a seventh grader who used Change.org to successfully petition the Motion Picture Association to change the rating on a movie about school bullying so students in her junior high would be allowed to see it.[4]

Not all acts of micro-activism will immediately result in a desired change. But regardless of the outcome, learning how to impact community issues using digital tools is an important skill to develop in and of itself. The ability to motivate others to act for good in a virtual space will be a significant (if not *the* significant) determining factor in the effectiveness of future civic leaders. Young people need to practice using tech to make a difference now, if they are going to be prepared to lead our society when they grow up.

Identifying Opportunities to Engage

A prerequisite for helping our kids become engaged digital citizens is modeling opportunities where we ourselves can use our access to the digital world to make a difference. In the physical world, I do this with my kids when I see a piece of trash on the ground at the park. I look for this opportunity because it gives me the chance to teach that even though it isn't our trash, we can make a shared place a little better by throwing it away. My hope is that modeling this action will help my kids apply that principle in circumstances far beyond cleaning a park. We need to do the same type of modeling in the virtual world. You are likely already using technology to make your community better, but to an outside observer (our kids), that's not as evident as picking up a piece of trash (Dad's just on his laptop again). Unless we are transparent about how we're using technology to be engaged digital citizens, the opportunity for modeling is lost. This can be as simple as saying "I'll be right there, I'm just posting information on Nextdoor about the blood drive at church next week." Or "I'm sending a message asking Chris if he needs anything because his wife was in the hospital. Do you want to see what I wrote?"

This means, of course, that we first have to actually be using technology to engage with our community ourselves. Several years ago, the Stanford d.school created a program to teach people how to be change makers in their communities.[5] The first step of that program was developing a "bias to action" mindset. The concept was that we could learn more and make a greater impact by just starting to do good things rather than by spending a long time analyzing or overthinking our approach. As with the piece of trash on the playground, we didn't need to do a study or write up an action plan; we just identified a need and immediately took a small but meaningful action. What might a bias-to-action mindset look like in the digital world? It might be noticing that a local food bank you follow on Facebook needs donations and posting a message online encouraging your followers to join you in contributing. It might be posting how you responded in a situation where you observed a racist or discriminatory act, to encourage others to do the same. When being engaged digital citizens, we should paraphrase a line from our friends at the Department of Homeland Security: "If you see something, [do] something."

In addition to modeling digital engagement, we should also expose our children to situations where they can discover their own opportunities to help. A fun approach to helping young kids become engaged digital citizens comes from Mary Jalland, a kindergarten teacher at Westquarter Primary School in Falkirk, Scotland. Her class has a pet (stuffed) elephant, Blue Ellie, that travels around to physical and digital communities and shares what she's "seeing" with the children. Through this process, they learn about communities they haven't visited and increase their awareness of important social issues.[6] On one trip, Blue Ellie shared the challenges of living in a part of the world that lacked proper sanitation infrastructure. The kindergartners practiced being engaged digital citizens by deciding how they could use digital tools to help do something about this problem. In this particular case, they created a video explaining how diseases can spread when sanitary toilets are not available and highlighting nongovernmental organizations that are working to bring sanitary water to more people.[7] In their video, they encouraged others to participate in toilet twinning, a movement to buy a "twin" for each toilet in your house that can be given to someone in an underserved community.[8]

There are countless ways for young people to use technology to be engaged digital citizens. Let's consider examples of three different types of digital engagement. First, we will look at crowdsourcing—joining forces with large numbers of people to make a outsized impact. Second, we will look at ways for youth to use tech to directly engage and serve in local communities, including their most important local community—their own family. And finally, we will look at using coding as a tool to develop new solutions to important problems.

Crowdsourcing Tough Problems

One of the powers of the digital world is that it allows us to join forces with others to make a difference in a problem that is simply too complex to solve on our own. Known as crowdsourcing, this approach can be an easy way to become part of a broad community of engaged digital citizens. Crowdsourcing makes sense for addressing problems that either are very difficult (e.g., curing cancer, slowing climate change, or stopping human trafficking) or simply exist on a large scale (e.g., fixing all of the cracks in city sidewalks that make them inaccessible to someone with a wheelchair). Here are some examples of crowdsourced solutions.

Transcribing History

Digital tools can give us unprecedented access to learn about important moments in our history as a human race or even the history of our individual families. However, for this to happen, the information must be available in a digital format. Many of the records of our history are still stored in paper notebooks, as artifacts in museums, or on gravestones and other physical landmarks that are not searchable. Indexing projects are a form of crowdsourcing that allow people worldwide to digitize important historical artifacts to make them searchable and discoverable online. These projects work by presenting an image of a historical record through an app and asking users to take a few minutes to type the descriptions of the records into a searchable database. Generally, the same record is given to multiple people to help catch and correct errors. The Smithsonian Institution has used this approach to digitize the descriptions of millions of physical artifacts in its collections (see transcription.si.edu). Using this same approach, Ancestry.com's world archives project asks engaged digital citizens to move important historical data, like immigration records or marriage certificates, into the digital world. Find A Grave crowdsources taking pictures of cemetery headstones so people can find where their ancestors were buried. With a little bit of supervision, taking pictures or scanning records is an easy way for a young person to join in the process of digitizing history.

Helping the Blind to See

Crowdsourcing can be used to serve other members of our physical and digital communities. Be My Eyes is an app that allows engaged digital citizens to make the world more accessible to people who are blind or have a low level of vision. The idea was developed by Hans

Jørgen Wiberg, a Danish furniture craftsman, who is visually impaired himself. When a blind friend told him that he used video calls to connect with family and friends who could help him with tasks he couldn't complete on his own, Wiberg got the idea for Be My Eyes. He decided to crowdsource the use of video technology to assist blind or low-vision individuals. The app connects a network of sighted volunteers to people with visual impairments through their mobile devices. If a blind person needs help with a particular task, say, reading the expiration date on a carton of milk or reading a phone number, they can connect with a sighted person through the app to have it read to them. Over 2 million volunteers are already participating in over 150 countries in over 180 languages to help people who are blind or have a low level of vision.[9]

Curbing Human Trafficking

The International Labor Organization estimates that over 40 million people globally are trafficked illegally and against their will.[10] To put that into perspective, that's about the population of the entire state of California. The problem has continued to elude law enforcement, as traffickers are careful to post pictures advertising their victims' services in virtual spaces where anonymity allows these acts to continue. TraffickCam is an initiative to use technology to crowdsource a solution. The request for digital citizens is simple: every time they stay in a hotel room, they take a picture of the room and upload it to Traffick-Cam's database.[11] Using artificial intelligence, unique elements of the rooms are identified (the pattern of the curtains, the distance between the TV and the wall, the color of the carpet, etc.). This creates a unique digital fingerprint of each room. These elements are then matched to the backgrounds of pictures posted on human trafficking sites. By comparing the unique elements of the images with the TraffickCam database, law enforcement officers can pinpoint hotels—even specific rooms—that are used by people who are being illegally trafficked. Your older teen could help in these efforts by snapping a few pictures of a hotel on their next vacation or school field trip.

Curing Disease

A final example of crowdsourcing can be seen in the fight to cure cancer. To understand how this works, it helps to dust off a bit of what we learned in high school about proteins. Proteins carry out a huge variety of jobs, including supporting a cell's structure, creating energy, sending messages, and repairing damaged DNA.[12] They are also part of diseases like Covid-19, AIDS, and cancer. What role protein will play is determined by its shape. Knowing how proteins are shaped or folded not only helps us figure out what a particular protein does, but also gives us a recipe book for creating new proteins that can be designed to combat our most serious illnesses. Because of the enormous variability in the way proteins can fold, identifying the many possible shapes had long been regarded as one of the hardest problems in science. But now, using a crowdsourced game called Foldit, people can compete with each other to identify new variations in the shape of proteins. Players get points every time they identify a new folding pattern, but the winner is science. Creating vaccines and even potential cures for diseases has been dramatically accelerated by more than two hundred thousand people worldwide who work together to supercharge the decoding. In one case, Foldit players helped identify the structure of the Mason-Pfizer monkey virus (M-PMV) that causes AIDS-like symptoms. This scientific problem had been unsolved for fifteen years, yet in ten days, Foldit players working together produced a 3D model of the enzyme that was accurate enough for molecular replacement.[13]

Serving in Their Communities

Some of the most important contributions young people can make come from opportunities to serve in their local communities. Let's look at some ways to use technology to mentor, serve, and encourage others to take action as well.

Being a Virtual Force for Good

Young people can use technology to encourage those around them to make better choices. This can be as simple as sharing inspirational thoughts and ideas to highlighting important causes via online channels—perhaps alerting friends to programs like No One Eats Alone or to participate in an antiracism demonstration. Awareness of ALS disease became greater when social media users helped the ice bucket challenge go viral in 2016. That online challenge generated an estimated $220 million for research and support of ALS.

Being a force for good can also be about shining the spotlight on other people whose voices need to be heard. In the summer of 2020 during the protests against racism in the US, social media users highlighted African American voices by retweeting and reposting their stories and by muting unrelated posts so they didn't stifle voices that needed to be heard. The things young people choose to stand for through their virtual presence, especially when combined with invitations to act, can amplify their impact in their communities.

Remote Reading Buddies

Several years ago, Eric Turner was working at an alternative school for fourth- to twelfth-grade students outside of Nashville. His students were serving time for issues of misconduct and were required to meet a certain number of service hours. Kory Graham was a kindergarten teacher in rural Dodge Center, Minnesota. Like all kindergarten teachers, she felt the pressure of making sure a bunch of hyper six-year-olds got enough reading practice, knowing that reading is a foundational skill that the rest of their academic success would depend on. Reading had to be fun. Turner and Graham hatched an idea for a digital service activity. Once a week, Turner's high school students would read to Graham's kindergartners via video chat. Turner's kids would prepare two books, and the kindergartners would choose which one they wanted to hear (though often they got to read both). This activity gave Turner's students a reason to practice reading, something many struggled with, and to experience the responsibility of being role models to younger kids who looked up to them, something the students had never felt before.

Turner recalls, "The students that read came out glowing—you could see the effect on them." The experience was similar for the kindergartners, too. "It was pure magic," Graham explains. "They felt so special that high school kids would take the time to read to them. I have goosebumps just thinking about it."[14] Turner remembers that one of his students was struggling to learn to speak English. Reading to the kindergartners became a new motivation for him to work on his language. He would practice and practice to make sure he could read the story well enough that the children could understand him.

Both teachers quickly realized that the benefits of this activity went far beyond literacy skills. Graham's students, living in a predominantly white community, had an opportunity to interact with Turner's diverse group of students, gaining an appreciation for people from different backgrounds. "We may have been reading to kindergartners, but we were also able to make friends with people who didn't look like us." And for Turner's students, technology provided an opportunity to serve and experience the positive feedback of contributing to other members of the community.

Connecting with Your Neighborhood

The digital world can be a great platform for strengthening connections to a young person's neighborhood community as well. In a world where we often don't know our neighbors' names, apps like Nextdoor help create a stronger feeling of community. A friend recently shared with me that a family in her neighborhood created an online newspaper produced by kids digitally as a way to keep in touch during the Covid-19 pandemic and as a way to make it more fun for kids to do their distance-learning writing assignments. Sites like JustServe.org also help us connect with members of our local community through service opportunities.

We can think creatively about ways to engage with our neighborhood community. Start by asking your kids what issues they want to help with, whether it's cleaning up the neighborhood, helping a local charity, or even spreading cheer in tough times. Technology can help connect their interests with opportunities to engage with others in your local community. And we can always use our digital presence to amplify important local events and causes via social media. Get your kids involved. They might surprise you with what they come up with.

Strengthening Family Relationships

Of all the communities our children participate in, their family is likely the most important of all. Engaged digital citizens know how to use their access to the digital world to deepen and strengthen ties to members of their families. As parents, we can model the use of digital tools for strengthening family relationships. You might try the following ideas in your own home.

Digital Family Councils

Members of my extended family are geographically dispersed across the country and might get to see each other in person only once a year. To strengthen family relationships, our family has established a tradition of holding monthly digital family councils. During a family council, everyone logs into Zoom; each family takes turns hosting. We start with a quick update on everyone and share accomplishments that have happened in that month. We talk about upcoming family events and challenges we may be facing so we can be aware of opportunities to help each other. Sometimes we have a parents-only family council to talk about issues that may not be appropriate for the kids to participate in (like advice on supporting a family member that is struggling). But even in those cases, we tell our kids that we're having a family council, so they learn the concept of using the virtual world to build family connections. In addition to the monthly family councils, we also use a family text thread and apps like Marco Polo to stay connected to each other. Technology is a powerful tool to strengthen and close the distance between physically dispersed families.

Capturing Family Experiences

One of my favorite ways for young people to practice being engaged digital citizens is by helping capture important family moments. When we take a family trip or celebrate a holiday, our kids can take the responsibility to preserve those memories. With a high-quality camera on almost every mobile device, children have the tools at their fingertips to be videographers and photographers. Younger children can borrow a parent's phone if they don't have their own device yet. In our family, the expectation of capturing family experiences is included as part of our children's device-use agreements. Free video- and photo-editing apps can turn photo and video collections into lasting stories. Beyond capturing photos and video, in our family we also have a tradition of recording funny moments. When a family member says or does something particularly funny, whoever was with them at the time writes down what happened on a shared notes app. At the end of the year, we create a "best of" collection of funny moments that we share with our family and friends. There are many special family memories that would have been lost if our kids had not taken on the responsibility of using their technology to capture these moments.

Preserving Family Stories

Robyn Fivush, a psychology professor and director of Emory University's Institute for the Liberal Arts, studies the surprisingly important role that family stories play in young people's lives. Her research shows that sharing family stories contributes to kids' emerging sense of self, both as an individual and as a member of their family. She says family stories teach children a sense of belonging. They provide

Starter Questions for Family History Interviews

We used the following questions for interviews with our children's great-grandparents. You can use them as a basis for capturing your own family stories or create your own list. You can record stories in person or via apps like Zoom. There are hundreds of audio and video editing apps to help create the final product.

- What was your weirdest job?

- What was your most embarrassing moment?

- How did you meet Grandma/Grandpa?

- What's your favorite thing about Grandma/Grandpa?

a script for life, and a set of values and guideposts.[15] In her research, Fivush found that adolescents who can recount details of family stories have higher self-esteem and greater resilience. She found that young people use stories told by parents to understand things about themselves. In one example, a teenager recalled a story about his mother standing up to a bully on behalf of another child. He ended the story saying, "That's why I always speak up for myself. Because my mother was so brave to do that." Through a family story, this teenager was learning something important about what type of person his mother is as well as an important moral lesson about the world.[16]

Technology enables kids to develop a deeper connection to their families while commemorating family history. Several years ago, we came up with a series of questions to ask our children's great-grandparents (see "Starter Questions for Family History Interviews") and recorded the audio of the interviews. These recordings preserve the stories of their great-grandparents and allow family members to continue to hear voices of relatives who have passed away. Sites like

- Who were your role models when you were a kid?

- What was life like growing up in your home?

- What's your favorite place that you've traveled to?

- Who was your best friend in school?

- What did you think you would be when you grew up?

- Did you serve in the military? If so, what did you do?

- Do you have any regrets looking back on your life?

- What's a tough decision you had to make and how did you decide?

- What are some important world events that took place in your lifetime?

Ancestry.com or FamilySearch.org are tools who can help tell a family's story by allowing kids to see who the earliest members of their family were, where they came from, and who else they are related to. Working together with my kids, we've learned about hundreds of our ancestors and found records showing when my Grandpa Sal came to the United States and even a picture of the boat he traveled on. As kids use digital tools to preserve the history of their families, they learn that they are part of something bigger than themselves, which provides a stronger foundation when challenges arise.

Coding: The Language of Problem-Solving

Up to this point, we have explored ways to use our access to the digital world to amplify voices of young people and join together to improve our global, local, and family communities. But there is one more skill that we might consider in order to prepare our kids to be successful digital citizens. We need to teach them the language of problem-solving in the digital world: coding. When I served as the chief innovation officer for Rhode Island, we set a goal to be the first state in the country to teach computer science in every school. The initiative received national attention for the community-based approach that led to meeting our goal in under eighteen months (record time for a significant change in public education). But the more important part of the story was the *why* behind the goal. Why would it be a top priority for a small New England state to make sure all children had the opportunity to learn to code, even if they had no interest in a future tech career?

Think for a moment about some of the challenges we face in our global community, both now and in the future. We need the ability to design and manufacture vaccines at a fast rate. We need to make education more accessible. We need a whole host of solutions to address environmental dangers that threaten our future on this planet. We need finance and banking solutions for areas of the world with limited infrastructure. We need new business opportunities to make sure the next generation of workers is prepared for the jobs of the future. The list, of course, goes on and on. Our issues and challenges are varied and complex. But the one constant across all these problems is that the solutions will be, in large part, found in computer code. Coding is the language of future problem-solving. States and countries that focus on teaching computational thinking will be the ones that have the greater capability to solve our future problems. Those that don't will find themselves increasingly dependent on others to do so.

As we teach the language of digital problem-solving, we need to include young people who may not immediately see value in learning to code. Traditional coding camps or school computer science classes have not had a great track record when it comes to including girls or African American and Latino youth. A research team at the University of Washington explored how uninviting computer science classrooms are and what can be done to make them better. It turns out, just removing some of the *Star Wars* posters from the walls and adding a few plants can make a surprising difference in making the space feel more welcoming. But most importantly, school guidance counselors and parents need to understand that learning to code isn't a skill reserved for geeky boys who want to go into computer programming jobs, but for *all* engaged digital citizens. If we only teach coding to a limited group of people, we will have dramatically limited our future problem-solving capabilities.

Around the world, engaged young people are already designing apps for tackling major challenges in their communities. Brittany Wenger was seventeen years old when she decided to teach a computer to diagnose brain cancer.[17] Saaket Jajodia and his brother, Salil, built an app to help their peers donate their time to good causes in their neighborhood in Bangalore.[18] When David Suhkin was in sixth grade, he built an app that would help predict the likelihood of a snow day being called the next day—hey, if you're a student, this is an important problem that needs to be solved.[19]

I recently visited Calipso High School in Cali, Colombia. The school is located in a socioeconomically challenged region and operates with very limited resources. But the principal, Alverio Velasco, understood the importance of preparing his students to be engaged digital citizens. He prioritized teaching computer science, not in an abstract way, but with the goal of helping students use tech to make the world around them better. During my visit, a group of students showed me a program they had designed to make public transportation safer through motion-detecting lighting at bus stops. Another student showed me an operating robotic hand he had designed and 3D-printed. He told me he designed the hand to help someone who had lost the physical ability to pick things up. The code for these projects was just a prototype, but the understanding that the students at Calipso were gaining about using code as a tool to improve their communities was very real.

Learning to Code and Hackathons

Of course, most young people don't figure out how to teach a computer to diagnose cancer while they're still in high school. The real break-throughs will likely come as they work together throughout their lives with other engaged digital citizens who also speak the shared language of digital problem-solving. But for that to happen, we need to prepare them with the basic skills now. Talk to your children's school counselors about what computer science classes are offered in their school. Apps like Lightbot, Scratch, or Tynker all teach coding in fun ways to get younger kids started with coding at home. Code.org's Hour of Code encourages kids to change the world through a variety of online coding activities. Girls Who Code and Black Girls Code are programs that offers coding experiences for girls worldwide.

For older children who already have an understanding of the basics of coding, a great way to start to practice using tech for good is by participating in computer problem-solving competitions known as hackathons. Hackathons are team challenges where students compete to use technology to solve a variety of problems in a short time (usually over a weekend). When I worked for President Obama, we hosted hackathons at the White House to look at issues ranging from designing tools to make it easier for first-generation college students to plan for college to helping families get easier access to their digital health-care records. In Rhode Island, instead of creating a single public transportation app, we provided access to a data feed with real-time locations of our city buses and invited developers, including student teams, to build apps to help Rhode Islanders more effectively navigate the public transportation system. The COVID-19 Global Hackathon had participants from 175 countries working together to tackle challenges related to the coronavirus pandemic. There is even a National Day of Civic Hacking sponsored by Code for America.[20] Searching on hackclub.com or blackgirlscode.com will show you hackathon and coding clubs that are happening in your region.

In summary, our kids are surrounded by innumerable opportunities to make their world a better place. They don't have to wait until they are older to begin to have an impact on the people around them. Fortunately, they have access to a more powerful tool set for community engagement than any generation before them. As parents, it's our job to help our children become comfortable making the connection between opportunities to be forces for good in their communities and the digital tools to help them do so. This is just as important when it comes to strengthening and connecting our families. In a virtual world, problems are solved in lines of code by people who know how to speak the language. As our children begin to understand the power of their digital devices to improve their virtual and physical spaces, they are also practicing the skills they need to become our future global leaders.

Next Steps

Action Items

- Model the use of technology to participate in micro-activism or crowdsourced problem-solving, and involve your children where appropriate.

- Brainstorm with your family about ways they can help their community by using social platforms and technology, including highlighting important causes or events.

- Create the habit of regular digital family interactions such as family councils or chats with faraway relatives (read books together, learn or teach a new skill, play a game, etc.).

- Talk to your school about coding programs that are offered. With your child, select a fun app, online program, or community group that teaches coding.

- Consider adding a few service-oriented digital activities as part of your device-use agreement.

- Search for famous people you may be related to by using Family-Search.org's famous relative Finder.

- Work with your kids to use technology to capture important family moments or stories.

Conversation Starters

- What is something you could do to help make the world around you a better place to live?

- Have you ever found an opportunity to help another person online?

- If you could solve one problem at your school, what would it be?

- How could you use technology to help you solve that problem?

- If you could invent a new app that would make the world better, what would it do?

- How can you help capture and preserve family experiences and stories?

7

Alert

Creating Safe Spaces Online

''ve already made the case that ensuring online safety is not the same as teaching digital citizenship, even though they frequently get confused. And while the concepts aren't interchangeable, the principles of online safety and privacy remain critical competencies of alert digital citizens. I prefer using the term "alert" when talking about online safety because it reminds us that staying safe online requires action and awareness; we keep our kids safe by teaching them to remain alert. Digital citizens not only keep themselves safe online but are also mindful of creating a safe space for others online as well.

I find the analogy of a nuclear power plant to be particularly useful in helping us become alert digital citizens. Nuclear energy is the largest source of clean power in the United States. Nuclear power plants keep 520 million metric tons of carbon from going into the atmosphere each year. That's the equivalent of removing 111 million cars from the road.[1] Yet they also have significant, associated risks, including being a target for terrorist attacks, suffering damage

Dangerous Behaviors
to Be Aware Of

In order to be alert to prevent dangers, parents need to be aware of the potential risks. The following are types of dangerous behaviors that can exist online that we should be alert for:

- Sending harassing texts or posts about a group or individual (known as "trolling")

- Finding and widely sharing personal information about someone to embarrass them (known as "doxing")

- Impersonating someone by figuring out the password to their social media account or setting up a new social media account that looks like theirs and making posts in their name

- Threatening to post actual or fake nude photographs in order to manipulate someone (known as "sextortion")

- Pretending to be an online romantic interest in order to manipulate or embarrass someone (known as "catfishing")

- Tricking someone into giving money or personal information via a fraudulent website or email (known as "phishing")

- Recruiting someone to believe in an extreme ideology or make risky decisions

- Buying or selling illegal substances or media online

- Sending nude or intimate selfies to another person (known as "sexting")

Some might brush off the last one since it is generally consensual. However, in many states, minors sending or taking intimate pictures is considered distribution of child pornography and has serious legal consequences. In addition, a digital trail of intimate media can trigger future digital manipulation should a relationship go sour.

from natural disasters, or dealing with employee mistakes that can cause costly damage or radiation leaks. In spite of these risks, nuclear plants in the United States have an impressive track record for safety, thanks to a range of protective measures in place to keep the plants safe. These safety strategies fall into three buckets. First are technical protections, including motion and temperature sensors, cameras, and alarms on every door that all send alerts when something is out of order. Second are the physical protections—anti-scaling fences around the perimeter, locks on the doors, armed security officers, and so on. Finally, there is training. Everyone who sets foot in a nuclear power plant, from the janitor to the CEO, must have the proper training on appropriate procedures for their job, how to avoid danger in the plant, and how to quickly spot and respond to anything that seems suspicious.

As the father of four children, trying to keep my own kids safe online feels a bit like trying to protect the nuclear power plant. It is much better to protect against potential dangers than try to repair them after the fact. Let's look at the three categories of nuclear power plant protections and explore how we can adapt each to strategies for keeping our family safe online.

Technical Protections

When it comes to online safety, the most fundamental technical protection is a web-filtering service. A web filter is software that identifies dangerous and inappropriate websites and blocks them from being accessed by computers and mobile devices on the network. A web filter can be added to any home Wi-Fi network so devices that connect to the internet are automatically protected as long as they are using your network. Services like Clean Browsing or OpenDNS are free network-filtering services that screen out the vast majority of violent and sexually explicit content. These services are easy to enable and provide step-by-step instructions on their sites. They require you to log in to your Wi-Fi network settings to enable. If you don't know how to do that, just give your internet provider a call and tell them you want to set up a web filter, a request they should be very familiar with.

A limitation to a web filter on your home Wi-Fi network is that it doesn't offer any protection when a device is connecting to the internet via another network (e.g., at friend's house or with a cell phone data plan). That's where a device filter comes in. These services allow you to set up an individual filter on each device, no matter what network it is using to connect to the internet. In addition to providing internet filtering, these services also allow you to set a variety of customized controls specific to each device. For example, you can set up blackout times when the device will no longer function (e.g., after bedtime) or receive alerts for activity that could be cyberbullying. There are many device filters available, including Circle (meetcircle.com) or Bark (bark.us). Device filters require paid subscriptions but are generally worth the cost. All of the major US wireless providers offer device-filtering services that can be added on to your existing plan for a few extra dollars a month.

Android and iOS devices have some built-in parental controls that are worth exploring as well. The most useful is the option for parental approval of apps before they are added to the phone. When enabled, a child will see "request" instead of "download" when they are in the device's app store. This sends the app request to designated approvers on the account to trigger a conversation before accepting or declining. Parental controls can be enabled in settings on Apple and Android devices.

Web filtering is the starting point for creating a safe environment for your family. But there are other technical protections you should also consider before letting your kids wander freely in the virtual world.

Access Is a Process, Not an Event

Another technical protection that can be easily implemented—yet is vastly underused—is the practice of limiting device functionality. Many parents think that device access is an all-or-nothing proposition. As a result, some kids' first experience with a smartphone comes with full access to all the digital features on their device—far too much responsibility for kids to gain in one shot. Being granted access to a device should be a gradual entrance to the digital world that happens over time. When it comes time to drive a car, we don't simply hand our kids the keys one day and send them on their way. Typically, they start learning navigation skills by first exploring the town on their bike. Then they practice driving a car in a parking lot. After taking Driver's Ed, we let them practice on the road, but only with an adult in the car and never after dark. Even once they get their license, it might be a year before we are comfortable allowing them to drive in a city or with friends in the car.

We should think about device access as similar to learning how to drive. In our family, when our kids first get access to devices (usually a hand-me-down phone or tablet of ours), we remove most of the apps on the device. We make it into the device-equivalent of learning to navigate with their bike before practicing driving a car. Our eight-year-old's "phone" has no data plan, no web browser, no YouTube app, and no social media access. There are a couple of fun games, a calculator, a clock, and the ability to take pictures and message other members of the family when on our home network. And because we have app approval enabled, no other apps can be added without a conversation. It's a bike, not a Tesla. Even though it may look like the same phone my teenage daughter has, the functionality is significantly limited. Over the course of several years, as our kids develop trust and experience, we gradually add functionality back to the device—turning on a web browser, adding YouTube, signing up for a data plan. The point here is that access to a phone is not a single event but a gradual experience that takes place over many years earned with growing maturity and trust.

Autoplay Is Not Your Friend

One technical protection important enough to deserve additional attention is autoplay. In the physical world, you would never allow a stranger to stop by your house, pick up your child, take them somewhere—anywhere—without knowing who they are or where they are going. Yet we do the virtual equivalent of that when we put our kids in front of an app with autoplay enabled. Yes, I know that I should probably be making organic playdough instead of having them watch *Pocoyo* in the first place, but there are many times when my sanity and my kid's safety are both better served if we all take a little movie break. But no matter how much of a break we need, we should *never* cede control of what our kids are watching to an algorithm that is optimized around the financial gain of the platform.

YouTube is particularly problematic in this regard. Since video creators only make money when their videos are played, many videos are designed to appeal more to YouTube's autoplay algorithms than to any human who might be watching. The process may use videos that are not even created by humans but by video-generating bots that know how to use the right keywords—videos that your kid would never purposefully choose to watch. This content may be inappropriate and shocking to children. In James Bridle's TED Talk, he shows how in just ten steps of autoplay, a child can go from a happy cartoon singing the ABCs to a horrible cartoon of sexualized Disney characters. Fortunately, the solution is simple: disable autoplay on any video service. YouTube, Disney+, and Netflix all now offer the ability to disable autoplay (even though Netflix was late to the party). So, take a video break, but don't hand over the controls for what your kids watch next to a bot. We should be intentional when it comes to the places our children visit online.

The False Security of Technical Protections

Technical protections, like the ones I've mentioned, are the easiest tools for keeping kids safe online. But we should be careful not to become overly confident in technical protections. Many parents and school leaders employ technical protections as their only strategy for keeping their kids safe. Every day, nearly 550,000 new websites are created. That's about 380 new websites per minute.[2] Every minute,

300 hours of new videos are uploaded to YouTube. At this staggering scale, even the best web filters can't possibly keep up with that amount of new digital material. Plus deciding what should be allowed through the filter can be trickier than it might seem. If we attempt to filter all pornographic sites by blocking the word "sex," we also block access to sites teaching about healthy sexual behavior and our kids' biology homework as well. If we block all sites with mature language, we inadvertently wipe out access to much literature and even parts of the Bible. When technical protections are so strict that they block reasonable use of the internet, kids are practically encouraged to find ways around the filters. As much as we might not want to admit it, there are always ways to get around even the best technical protections.

But the real danger in relying only on technical protections is that they don't require any effort on the part of the humans using the networks. We will have done nothing to prepare our kids for how to handle the inevitable moment when they do encounter something inappropriate online. We should never think that adding technical protections absolves us of the responsibility of teaching budding digital citizens the skills they need to be alert online. For those skills, we need to return to the other two parts of the nuclear power plant analogy.

Physical Protections

The second set of strategies for protecting a nuclear power plant are physical protections. These require no tech skills to implement or software to configure. When keeping our kids safe online, the best physical protection is establishing locations where digital device use is appropriate and where it is not. Schools and recreation centers often establish locker rooms as device-free zones for obvious reasons. But there are other physical locations we should add to the list. In our family, we have a simple expectation that when you have a digital device in your room, the door must stay open. We establish this habit from the moment our kids first start using their devices. It is an easy way to teach the concept that moments that require the privacy to shut the door (e.g., changing clothes, etc.) are also moments when devices should feel out of place. By making that connection at an early age, when kids become teenagers, they have a natural instinct to leave the door open if the device is on. This simple habit removes the conditions required for a variety of problematic activities to occur.

Another example of physical protection comes in the placement of computers. A family desktop placed in the back corner of a basement room is as much a recipe for disaster as building a nuclear power plant and not bothering to put a fence around the perimeter. A better place for a family computer might be in a desk area in the kitchen or other well-trafficked location, positioned so the screen faces into the room. If a computer must be in a child's room for school or because no common area is available, set it up so the screen is facing the door. It's much harder to have cyberbullying go unnoticed when others can see what is on the screen. A final example of a physical protection is to turn in mobile devices, including laptops, at the end of the day. As I mentioned previously, in our family, all mobile devices sleep on a table in the corner of our bedroom. Keeping devices in another room overnight allows for uninterrupted sleep and also removes conditions for risky activities.

Training Protections

Just like the training workers receive before entering the power plant, training protects members of our family from potential dangers in the virtual world. The most important takeaway from this section is to do our best to establish an open dialogue about the experiences our kids are having online. We should have ongoing conversations about where our kids go and what they do in the physical world. Just as we might ask, "What did you do at James's house?" when our kids come back from visiting a friend, we might ask, "What's happening on SnapChat today?" or "What interesting ideas have you added to your Pinterest board recently?" when our kids come back from visiting virtual spaces. Ongoing dialogue provides a channel for addressing a variety of issues that may arise.

Media literacy professor Renee Hobbs suggests that when parents participate with their children in online spaces, it is easier to have a dialogue about what's happening there. The purpose in going with kids online is not to control their behavior but to develop the context in which to mentor them in navigating those spaces safely and effectively. It becomes a chance to help young people evaluate their virtual presence and determine if it is really what they want it to be.

Joint participation with kids in virtual spaces is also a great learning opportunity for parents who are less familiar with the virtual world. We might ask our kids to teach us how to build something in *Minecraft* or ask older kids to share the five funniest posts they've seen on TikTok. We could have a friendly competition to see who can take the most creative picture in a week or find the most interesting YouTube video. Or we might get advice from our kids about how to use technology to address a problem we're trying to solve at home or work. And just because we may not consider ourselves tech-savvy doesn't mean we still don't have value to add. We should be careful not to conflate our children's tech skill with tech literacy. Just because a young person knows the logistics of using technology doesn't mean they know how to conduct themselves appropriately in virtual spaces.

In addition to establishing ongoing conversations with our kids about their activities in the virtual world, there are three ideas that I recommend teaching young people to help them stay alert.

1. Not Everyone Is Trustworthy

A basic training concept that every digital citizen must learn is that not everyone in the virtual world is trustworthy. We already teach this in the physical world—don't talk to strangers, don't get into the car of someone you don't know, and so on. But in the online world, we must also remember to teach about an additional twist. Not being trustworthy can also mean not being truthful about who someone appears to be. A young person can find it difficult to believe that a fifteen-year-old girl from New York posting to Instagram may actually be a forty-five-year-old guy from India. In the physical world, we use a person's identity as a reliable indication of the level of trust we should have in them. When we use this approach to establish trust online, where it is easy to fabricate an identity, we can easily get into trouble. This also includes the possibility of interacting with someone who we know (a friend from school who we have been texting for years) but has had their profile compromised. We should prepare our kids to be alert for the signs that a friend's account may have been hacked, such as:

- Asking questions that don't seem in line with what they would normally ask about (e.g., "remind me of your address" or "remind me how we met")

- Having an "emergency" and needing money or information sent immediately

- Being unwilling to discuss the issue on another platform (by phone, text, etc.)

- Asking for inappropriate pictures or personal data

In any situation, when our kids have a concern about the trustworthiness or identity of an online individual, we encourage them to come talk to us.

2. Some Virtual Spaces Are Riskier Than Others

The second concept is that just like in the physical world, some places in the virtual world are safer than others. We should arm our kids with some indications to look for to determine whether a virtual space is safe. For websites, this includes looking for the lock icon on the top right of the URL in your browser, which indicates that the site has been verified by a third party. Or, for an app, you might check out a review from Common Sense Media. Some signs indicate that a site or app may be unsafe, including obvious spelling or grammatical errors, a request that you download software or save a file, or the forced opening of multiple browser windows. We should be particularly alert to anything about the URL that seems unusual (e.g., yah00. com or amazon.net).

Some segments of the internet are riskier than others. If you think about the web as an ocean, most of the web that you've likely experienced is in the first hundred feet. It's where familiar websites with URLs ending in .com, .org, and .gov live. This surface web is the part of the internet that Google searches. But below that level, there is another part of the internet known as the deep or dark web. Typically, sites there end in .onion, and you generally have to use a special web browser (like Tor) to get around. That part of the web allows you to buy services like renting a hacker to mess up someone's online identity or buying knockoff prescription medication. It is also where personal information skimmed from the surface web is sold and traded. Your kids are unlikely to stumble into the dark web by accident but we need to be aware that back alleys exist online; we should teach them that they should avoid any sites that promote sketchy activities. The chief learning officer of the International Society for Technology in Education, Joseph South, recommends teaching our kids to simply ask, "How does the site or app make you feel?" If you're feeling that something isn't right, don't wait around for extra confirmation; just leave.

3. Recognize the Value of Personal Information

Personally identifiable information (or PII, as it's known) is any data that makes it possible to identify someone individually. PII includes the obvious things like name, address, and phone number. But it can also include information like medical history, online purchases, or school class schedules. Alert digital citizens know to be careful not to share PII with someone who is not trustworthy. We might choose to share some PII when signing up for a new online account. But if we're not careful, we can share it in unintended ways as well, like posting a photo that happens to have a house number in the background or by using an unsecure Wi-Fi network. There are many ways to trick us into sharing PII, such as taking a seemingly innocuous online personality quiz that includes a question like "What is your mother's maiden name?" or "What street did you grow up on?" (items that are commonly used as security questions on our online accounts).

PII is extremely valuable to companies in the virtual world, often more so than cash. If a company uses advertising to get us to buy a single product, it will earn a small amount of money. But if a company can get our PII, it can create a customized sales channel optimized to get many sales over the course of many years. In other words, our personal information is a currency that can be exchanged for cash at a very favorable exchange rate. And that's assuming the intent of the person obtaining our PII is on the up-and-up. On the dark web, PII can be traded and sold for financial gain or for the intent of damaging someone's reputation.

We need to make sure our children understand that when they enter their personal information to get a "free" app or service, they are still paying for it, but with PII instead of cash. It might be worth the price, but it's never free. As NYU business professor Scott Galloway points out, "The cost of using Amazon Alexa is the use of your data to make their online store more profitable. Amazon's customers trust it so much that they're allowing the company to listen in on their conversations and harvest their consumption data."[3] Alert digital citizens understand the value of their personal data. They know how to evaluate whether the return on investment of the services they are receiving is worth paying with this valuable currency of personal data.

Spotting a Safety Violation

Just as we should be aware of the different types of digital harassment, we should also be aware of the signs indicating dangerous behaviors might be occurring. The following are some common indicators compiled from the Anti-Defamation League and Cyberbullying.org that we should watch for.[4] We should pay particular attention anytime a young person:

- Becomes upset, sad, or angry during or after being online or using their phone

- Withdraws from family or friends

- Doesn't want to participate in activities they previously enjoyed

- Doesn't want to go to school or a specific class

- Changes screens whenever you walk by or only wants to use the computer in a private place

- Seems nervous or jumpy when they get an instant message, text, or email

- Has changes in eating or sleeping habits

If you suspect that your child is involved in any sort of unhealthy online activity, you might be tempted to freak out, destroy their devices, and lock them in a safe room for the rest of their lives. Unfortunately, that is never the best approach. Resolving inappropriate digital interactions requires maintaining a trusting relationship and open dialogue with your kids. Remain as calm as possible when talking about whether or not dangerous behaviors may be happening. If you address them quickly, you can resolve the vast majority of issues before there are serious consequences. However, if a child is afraid of your reaction and chooses to hide a dangerous behavior, the consequences could become more serious during the months or years that the behavior remains unaddressed. If there is a situation where digital abuse is occurring, don't respond or retaliate against the offender. That may seem counterintuitive, but often getting that reaction is the very goal of the offender.

There are helpful actions to take if a dangerous digital behavior is happening. If someone is bothering your child in a virtual space, use tools to block them so additional messages don't come through. If the harassment is happening on a social media platform, you should flag the inappropriate behavior. For information on how to do that for each major media platform, go to cyberbullying.org/report. Save copies of inappropriate messages or posts as evidence, should the situation ever escalate. Talk to your child about anything they may have done that could make them a target, such as posting personal information in a public space, sending compromising pictures, or participating in harassing behaviors themselves. This is not to point the finger at your child but to get a full picture of the situation. If the dangerous behaviors involve other students, alert a school counselor or administrator. Finally, if there are physical threats or illegal behaviors, contact the police.

Training our kids that not everyone in virtual spaces is trustworthy, not every place is safe, and our personal data should be safeguarded are key elements of protecting them from online risks. Combined with technical and physical protections, alert digital citizens can take advantage of the opportunities of the virtual world while keeping themselves and others safe. When something does go wrong, having an open dialogue allows a quick and supportive response. As in the nuclear power plant, errors happen, but with multiple layers of appropriate protections in place, a quick intervention can resolve almost any situation before a serious problem occurs.

Next Steps

Action Items

- Select an internet or device filter depending on what makes most sense for your children. (For younger children who only use the internet at home, an internet filter may be all that is needed. For older children who take their devices outside the home, device filters may make more sense.)

- Start small. Don't give your child full access to every app or functionality when they first get their own device.

- Set up physical device protections, such as establishing an open-door device rule, placing shared computers in high-traffic spaces, and designating a night-time device-charging station.

- Disable autoplay on any video streaming service, such as YouTube or Netflix.

- Spend some time with your kids becoming more familiar with their favorite virtual activities.

- Keep an eye out for any warning signs that your child may be in danger.

Conversation Starters

- What should you do if you ever feel uncomfortable with something someone was asking you to do online?

- Have you ever seen someone pick on someone else online?

- What might you do when you see someone being mean to someone else online?

- What are some warning signs that a website or app might be unsafe?

- Who are your favorite people to follow on YouTube, TikTok, and so on, and what do you like about them?

- Would you feel comfortable coming to tell me if you felt worried about something you saw online?

- What are some things we should do as a family to protect us during our time online?

8

Digital Well-Being
Is a Team Sport

When we think about the physical well-being of our families, many responsibilities fall on the shoulders of parents. And while our responsibilities to keep our kids healthy are significant, we know we don't have to go it alone. We're part of a broader team of people and organizations that are working together toward that same goal. We teach our kids to evacuate a burning building safely, but we also expect that buildings are designed with working fire exits and that trained firefighters can control the flames. We make sure our kids wear seatbelts, but we also expect cars to have airbags and pass federal collision safety requirements. Doctors step in to help when our kids get sick; public works crews make sure the water we drink is sanitary. Police work to keep our communities safe; schools help prepare our children for future studies and careers.

As we think about our children's digital well-being, some key responsibilities are borne by parents—we've spent most of this book talking about them. But it would be disingenuous to assume that all of the responsibility for creating healthy digital citizens should be on families alone. Digital well-being is a community effort. We need a team of players, all bringing their talents to bear—a support system of experts that parents can partner with and trust. Understanding the roles (or potential roles) of the other team players is important for parents' awareness and also helps hold all team members' proverbial feet to the fire. As parents, our expectations can become a self-fulfilling prophecy for whether or not the other team roles are completed.

With that in mind, let's meet some of the other members of the team. We will also look at opportunities to advocate and ask those team members to do more to ensure the digital well-being of our children. There are hundreds of different roles that could form part of our extended digital citizenship team, but for practicality, we will look at the three key players: tech providers, governments, and schools.

Digital Platform Providers

We'll start with the most obvious member of the team, the tech providers themselves. Despite providing the tools that enable many of our digital dysfunctions, most digital platform providers have a vested interest in creating healthy digital citizens—for self-preservation, if nothing else. Responsible digital platforms have processes to report disconcerting activities. Facebook has been working to improve this process by expanding its "flag as inappropriate" option to identify a variety of potentially disconcerting behaviors, such as those suggesting self-harm, misinformation, hate speech, and so on. Facebook and other digital platforms depend on us to use these tools when we observe activities that we feel are problematic.

But digital platform providers need to do more to support our digital citizenship team effort. Author and entrepreneur Eli Pariser says we should expect more from our digital platform providers in exchange for the power we give them over our discourse. He believes we should ask not just how we make digital tools user-friendly, but also how we make digital tools *public*-friendly. In other words, it's our responsibility to make sure our digital platforms never serve individuals at the expense of the social fabric on which we all depend. With that in mind, let's look at three key responsibilities we should expect of our digital platform providers.

Establish Meaningful Norms

We should expect our virtual platforms, as members of our digital citizenship team, to establish and clearly communicate standards for participation in our virtual spaces. Some already do a good job of this, including Flickr, Lonely Planet, and The Verge. Flickr's community norms are simple, readable guidelines that are clearly designed for community members, not just lawyers, to understand.[1] They include some clear "dos" like:

> "Play nice. We're a global community of many types of people, who all have the right to feel comfortable and who may not think what you think, believe what you believe, or see what you see. So, be polite and respectful in your interactions with other members."

And they also include some clear "don'ts," like:

> "Don't be creepy. You know the guy. Don't be that guy. If you are that guy, your account will be deleted."

We should expect *all* of our digital platforms to establish a clear code of conduct. And we should expect it to be actively embedded throughout the virtual space. Even the examples I mentioned have their norms pretty deeply buried in the back corner of their sites. In chapter 2, I talked about the idea of sign-posting—creating messages and reminders of the norms of behavior for our physical shared spaces. A similar approach should be an expectation for our virtual platforms as well. Imagine if, instead of one more ad

Example of posting online norms in social media feeds

for new socks on Pinterest, a reminder appeared to "post something kind about someone else today." Or imagine if, instead of poking my eyes out from watching yet another Geico ad before a YouTube video plays, we might be presented with tips for how to respectfully disagree with the content of someone else's video. Sure, this would cause the platform providers to give up a fraction of a percentage of advertising revenue, but that's a very reasonable expectation for them to remain a trusted member of the team.

Verify Human Users

A second expectation of our platform providers is that they take more seriously the responsibility of identifying the users of their platforms that are not human. Most people would be shocked to learn how many of the "people" we engage with in virtual spaces are actually robots ("bots") designed to create highly reactive content. Some of the most divisive posts that flood the virtual world each day are generated by these bots, which are capable of arguing their digital positions with unsuspecting humans for hours on end.[2] One study found that during the height of the Covid-19 pandemic, nearly half of the accounts tweeting about the virus were bots.[3] YouTube and Facebook both have about as many robot users as human users.[4] Last year, Face-book removed over 2 billion fake accounts, but until additional veri-fication is added, new accounts will be created, also by bots, almost as quickly as the old ones are removed.[5]

In addition to clearly labeling bots as bots, platform providers should do more to verify the identity of human users as well, partic-ularly those that are widely followed. Many of the dark and creepy parts of our virtual world exist because online platforms have been irresponsibly lax in verifying that users are who they say they are. This doesn't mean platforms couldn't still allow anonymous users, but such accounts should be clearly labeled as unverified so that when your "neighbor" asks your daughter for information about her school online, she can quickly recognize if she should be suspicious. The technology to do this sort of verification exists and is fairly straight-forward (banks and airlines use it all the time). Twitter piloted this approach—you may have seen the little blue checkmarks next to some people's accounts—but then stopped, claiming it didn't have the bandwidth to continue. The lack of expectation for verified identities enables fraud, cyberbullying, and misinformation. If digital platforms want us to trust them to be the host of our virtual communities, we should expect them to identify and call out users who are not who they say they are.

Improve Content Curation

The third responsibility of our digital platform team members is to be more proactive in curating the content on their platforms. This starts with quickly addressing posts that incite racism, violence, terrorist activity, or features that facilitate buying illegal drugs, participating in identity theft, or human trafficking. Twitter recently began adding warning labels to bullying or misleading tweets from political leaders.[6] A notable example is when a tweet from Donald Trump was flagged for claiming that mail-in ballots lead to widespread voter fraud (for the record, there is absolutely no evidence that mail-in ballots are any more susceptible to voter fraud than in-person ballots). Apple has also taken this responsibility seriously with a rigorous review process on apps that are added to its mobile devices. Unlike the web, Apple does not permit apps that distribute porn, encourage consumption of illegal drugs, or encourage minors to consume alcohol or smoke on its devices. Apple and Google have both begun requiring apps on their respective stores to have content-moderation plans in place in order to remain.[7]

Effective content moderating also means doing more to empower human moderators. Reddit and Wikipedia are the largest examples of platforms that rely on human moderators to make sure their community experiences are in line with their established norms. In both cases, humans are not just playing a policing role, but taking an active part in developing the content on the platform. Both rely on volunteer curators, but we could reasonably expect human moderators to be compensated for their time and energy in making virtual community spaces more effective. This can be done in a variety of ways. YouTube currently incentivizes its content creators to upload videos to its platform by offering them a percentage of advertising revenue. A similar incentive could be given to encourage users who help curate the content on these platforms. This is very different from YouTube's current approach, which uses bots to moderate and curate. As author and technologist James Bridle points out, content on YouTube that is created by bots is also policed by bots, meaning robots are convincing other robots that their content should be viewed, and the human users of the platform are left paying the price.

Another simple way to empower users as moderators is to provide more nuanced options for reacting to each other's content. Right now, "liking" or "disliking" are about all the options we have to respond to content on shared platforms. Some platforms have added a happy face, a heart, and most recently a hug, but that is still an incredibly limited set of response options for the variety of content flowing around our digital world. In the physical world, soft-negative feedback is a critical tool for helping people learn the norms of community space. Most of the feedback we give in the physical world is much more subtle than what we can do online. If you were in a conversation with someone who said their kids were not going to get a vaccine because it contains a secret tracking microchip, we might respond with an "I don't know about that" or a "hmmm, I think you might want to check your facts." But in the virtual world, our only option might be to click the "thumbs down" button. In a world where very subtle reactions carry great significance, giving a big "thumbs down" to a friend is like the social equivalent of a full frontal assault. On the other hand, if you choose to sidestep the awkward moment by unfollowing your friend, you have just made sure they never hear your feedback again, likely reducing their sounding-board pool to people with similar views, which is even less helpful for establishing shared societal norms. What if instead of just "liking" or "disliking," we could tag things as "I question the source of this post" or "I love you, but I still disagree with you" or "that's a pretty extreme viewpoint."

Digital platform providers care what parents think; their continued existence depends on our continued trust. We should expect digital platforms to establish and clearly infuse their environments with media that teach appropriate norms of behavior on their digital spaces. We should call for them to do a better job of clearly labeling nonhuman users of their platforms and to empower their users to be more involved in content curation. Sending this message is as simple as sharing our needs with the platforms themselves (they all have forms to share feedback) or reaching out to the elected leaders who oversee them.

Local and Federal Government

Government, the next member of our digital citizenship team, plays a critical role by protecting and providing. Protection means keeping citizens safe from each other and external threats. Driving laws reduce accidents; diplomacy (and military strategy if necessary) keeps us safe from foreign attacks. And government provides the means to make sure citizens have access to the services they cannot reasonably provide for themselves including access to transportation, health care, quality schools, and commercial goods and services. The nuances of where and how the government accomplishes its role should be a topic of ongoing debate as it continually adapts and adjusts to the evolving needs of citizens.

As we become increasingly dependent on the digital world for many critical functions of our democracy and livelihood, we should expect the government to carry out its role to protect and provide in virtual spaces as well. Governments worldwide are beginning to step up to this responsibility. The European Union, Brazil, Japan, and Australia have recently made sweeping changes to protect their citizens from having their private information stolen online. EU leaders are currently pursuing new laws that keep companies like Amazon and Apple from giving their own products preferential treatment over their competitors' in their online stores in order to keep healthy competition in the digital marketplace. In Britain, officials are drawing up laws to ensure Facebook and Google play better in the sandbox with smaller competitors.[8] But government efforts to date have largely prioritized improving online business practices over creating healthy online environments for digital citizens. We need to call on our government leaders to exercise their responsibility in creating safe digital spaces for our families. The following are three specific opportunities around which we can call on government leaders to take action.

Provide Oversight for Digital Spaces

Governments have created stringent expectations that traditional media companies must comply with. This means we don't have to worry about our children seeing graphic sexual content or hearing profanity while watching TV. In response to an infamous wardrobe malfunction involving Janet Jackson and Justin Timberlake during a Super Bowl halftime show, the US Broadcast Decency

Enforcement Act established fines for media companies that violate the rules. The FCC also enforces guidelines—known as "KidVid rules"—that require broadcasters to include at least 150 hours of child-appropriate programming as part of their core schedule. And media companies that enable the sharing of illegal or defamatory information can be held liable. If a guest on CNN engages in hate speech or the *New York Times* publishes illegal content on its site, even if it's written by a guest author, the company is legally responsible. It seems reasonable for laws to require these organizations to remove hate speech and posts that deliberately incite violence or encourage terrorism.

But this oversight does not apply in the digital world. Internet-based media platforms like YouTube, Netflix, and Facebook can ignore these requirements, despite the fact that they have become our primary source of media. The loophole applies to online information-sharing sites as well. US Code 47 section 230 exempts websites from responsibility for content shared by users on their platform, even if it is defamatory or incites violence. But steps can be taken to close these loopholes. For example, in 2018, Section 230 was amended to make virtual spaces liable for enabling human sex trafficking—shuttering sites like backpage.com and removing the sex forums from Craigslist. Why not also make online platforms responsible for complying with the same standards as traditional media companies? This might include ensuring that a balance of media is offered in suggested playlists, hateful or violent media is removed, clear warning labels appear on graphic content, and controls are available for parents to limit the types of media shown to their children. It doesn't make any sense for traditional media companies to perform against a set of expectations while allowing new media platforms to completely sidestep them just because we haven't been diligent about keeping our laws caught up with advances in technology.

Ironically, the only legal requirement aimed at protecting children from harmful online media in the United States is the Children's

Internet Protection Act (CIPA). And in a textbook example of twisted logic, CIPA puts almost all of the responsibility on schools and libraries to figure out how to filter obscene images, child pornography, and other blatantly sexual content and no responsibility on the platforms providing that content in the first place. Not only do schools already have enough on their plate, but most individual schools don't have the technical chops or scale to shift the behaviors of major tech providers.

Other countries are beginning to take this role more seriously. Sweden, Norway, Denmark, and Belgium, for example, have all created guidelines that restrict digital advertising targeting children younger than twelve.[9] In the same way the government has taken its role as protector seriously in physical spaces, we should expect it to also take this role seriously in the digital world by establishing and enforcing consistent standards across all types of media platforms.

Ensure Equity of Access

A second key area where government needs to support parents in ensuring digital well-being is in equity of access. You can't become an effective digital citizen if you are excluded from the digital world. For almost a century, we have considered access to water, electricity, and phone service essential to a healthy life, not optional luxuries. As such, we have made it a priority to ensure all citizens have access to these basic utilities. If left to natural market forces alone, the availability of basic utilities would be highly inequitable.

Take electricity, for example. The cost to have electricity delivered to my house in a neighborhood in suburban Virginia is relatively low. But for someone living on a farm in Iowa or the Native American reservation in Alaska, the cost per home for providing electricity is prohibitively expensive. Without government involvement, there would be many parts of the country where it would just never be commercially viable to provide electricity. As part of the Great Depression Recovery Plan, the United States set an ambitious goal to make sure electricity was considered a basic utility that was available to all citizens regardless of whether they lived in highly dense or remote communities. Governments can do this in a number of ways, including:

- Offering access to government land (under streets, space on utility poles, etc.) to a utility provider to build their infrastructure in exchange for providing service to remote areas

- Providing grants to cover the capital expenditure for bringing utilities to remote locations

- Becoming a utility provider itself in areas where having a commercial provider just doesn't make economic sense

In addition, governments can create a variety of support services to help struggling families afford monthly utility costs. Programs like the Low Income Home Energy Assistance Program (known as LIHEAP) assist families with energy costs to ensure heat is available in the winter and cooling in the summer. Many states have their own energy assistance programs to supplement LIHEAP.

It's *long* past time to consider access to the internet a basic utility. As education, banking, health care, voting, and many other critical services migrate online, it is nearly impossible to be a functioning member of society without having access to the digital world. Fifty-five million people in the United States do not have a computer at home, and tens of millions of households do not have enough computers to allow for concurrent use by multiple family members. Individuals in these nondeviced or device-deficient households are often unable to access education, telehealth, and employment. Possessing a functioning, connected computer and the skills to use it productively is a basic, fundamental need in today's society. Even applying for an entry-level job at Walmart or Target is not possible without access to the internet. During the Covid-19 pandemic, lack of internet access also meant lack of access to public education, as schools moved to learning online.

In 2016, the United Nations passed a resolution declaring internet access a basic human right.[10] Universal internet service is already provided in Switzerland, Finland, Spain, and the UK. Uruguay provides a computer and connectivity to every student as they enter public school. The United States lags behind the rest of the developed world in terms of treating access to the virtual world like a utility. Fortunately, the same strategies used to make sure everyone has access to electricity and water also apply to accessing the internet, so it's a well-paved path if we are willing to make the case for elected leaders to make it a priority.

Protect Our Digital Privacy

Finally, government has a role to play in protecting our digital privacy. In the United States, the Health Insurance Portability and Accountability Act (HIPAA) sets boundaries on the use and release of digital health records and requires access controls and audit logs from providers to protect the information. It holds violators accountable, with serious penalties that can be imposed if they violate a patient's privacy rights. Beyond medical records, there is really no guidance to uphold the promise of privacy in other parts of the digital world in the United States.

Other countries have begun taking action though. In 2018, the European Union implemented the General Data Protection Regulation (known as GDPR) with the primary goal of giving citizens control of their personal data. This regulation applies to any company holding data about any EU resident regardless of the company's location. And, it turns out, the EU isn't messing around. Penalties for noncompliance are up to 4 percent of a company's annual global turnover—a big stick. Brazil, Australia, and Japan have followed suit to create their own similar data privacy regulations.

Creating laws that ensure our basic privacies online should be table stakes in a digital world where participation is no longer optional to remain a functioning member of society. We need a regulatory context that protects our data from being used and sold without our consent and a pathway for appropriate compensation when we do. In "Blueprint for a Better Digital Society," Jaron

Lanier and E. Glen Weyl propose the idea of data dignity, where the government would protect our right to own the data that exists about us now and forever.[11] This means when our data is sold to digital advertisers, we would get a royalty payment over time as the data is used. Lanier and Weyl estimate that a family of four could earn up to $20,000 a year from the royalties paid on the use of their data. This approach would not only bring additional transparency to what data of ours is being used but also allow *all* parties to benefit financially from its use.

To be an effective team player when creating a healthy digital environment for our children, government leaders need to move from reactive to proactive mode. Citizen voice matters to elected officials. If we want digital well-being to be a priority to them, we must make it clear that it is important to us. We should actively call on our elected leaders to fulfill their responsibilities to protect and provide in the digital world.

Schools and Universities

Our most important partners in teaching digital citizenship are our children's schools. Throughout their time in school, our kids benefit from teachers and coaches who provide guidance and have deep expertise that helps reinforce the concepts we're teaching at home. As members of our digital citizenship team, schools and universities have the important role of preparing the next generation of effective digital citizens, and also of preparing the future designers and builders of our digital platforms themselves.

Teaching Digital Citizenship in Schools

We should expect schools to closely collaborate with parents to support digital well-being. Many of the ideas presented in this book so far apply equally to teachers and other youth leaders, but I will add a few notes specific to schools here. First, teaching digital citizenship in school is not about creating a new class. It's about creating a new culture. The five attributes of effective digital citizens need to be modeled by teachers and school leaders and embedded into activities across *all* subjects. The Los Angeles Unified School District has used the five attributes presented in this book as a common framework and language to help its 35,000 teachers start a new conversation with their students. In particular, the elements of creating informed and engaged digital learners are particularly aligned to the responsibilities of schools. Every school should have a plan for how it will use technology to enable and support its core learning vision. Schools should establish ways to highlight and recognize students who demonstrate the attributes of digital citizens.

Parents can play a critical role in helping schools fulfill their responsibility in this area. A simple and helpful action that parents can take is to ask school leaders how they are teaching digital citizenship. If there is no plan or if the current approach is overly focused on online safety but missing other elements of digital citizenship, work with school leaders or the PTA to suggest some changes. Ask to see a copy of the school's acceptable-use policy for devices. If the policy is not written in language that is appropriate for youth or only includes things *not* to do, ask to organize a group of parents to make some recommended changes.

Preparing effective digital citizens is a responsibility of higher-education institutions as well. Two years ago, University of Washington professors Carl Bergstrom and Jevin West were concerned that their institution wasn't doing enough to prepare their students to recognize or respond to digital misinformation. They began offering a course called Calling Bullshit in the Age of Big Data, focused on detecting and addressing false information.[12] The class explores common misinformation traps, including misleading advertising, data visualization, and statistical tricks, and provides strategies for respectfully responding to people who intentionally or unintentionally spread it. Bergstrom and West believe that for the safety of our future society, the skill of recognizing and addressing BS is one of the most important skills any student needs to learn at college.

Unfortunately, the University of Washington is an outlier when it comes to explicitly teaching principles of digital citizenship. When you consider that you can take a course on tree climbing (Cornell University), whether or not Harry Potter is real (Appalachian State University), walking as a form of art (Centre College), and embracing distraction (Belmont University), it seems reasonable to expect more colleges to also prepare students to be effective members of our digital world. Oh, and if you worry that students aren't interested in the topic, the first semester the University of Washington course was taught, the 160-seat course limit was reached after one minute of the opening of registration.[13]

Preparing Future Designers

A second, less obvious but equally important responsibility of our education partners is to train the future designers and engineers who will build the platforms of our digital world. If we really want to have virtual spaces designed around supporting humanity and democracy, we need a generation of designers and developers who think differently about what they're creating.

For several years, I've served as a design resident for the global design firm IDEO. You may have never heard of IDEO, but the products they design likely fill your house under the names of a thousand brands. IDEO designed the first widely manufactured Apple mouse. If you have a toothbrush with that nice rubberized grip, you can thank IDEO for that, too. IDEO has become successful because their design philosophy is to obsessively keep the needs of people first and foremost when designing products and services. Its core design principle is empathy for the users. In the case of the toothbrush, the designers observed that when people used smooth, flat toothbrush handles with wet hands, the brush often slipped or people dropped it (and everyone hates using a toothbrush that has just dropped on the floor or in the sink). So IDEO designed around that problem. If a toothbrush has a rubber grip, it's much easier for human hands to hold. Now, almost every toothbrush has one. The process of designing for the needs of people has become known as human-centered design.

Today's digital platforms are often designed to prioritize advertising opportunities or number of downloads over the needs of the people and communities who use them. We could take a page from IDEO's book when training future designers. We need schools and universities to prepare developers and engineers who know how to keep humans (and humanity) at the center. This means teaching strategies to understand the societal impacts of the features that we build. For our schools and universities, this means rethinking our approach to teaching coding, business, and engineering. Traditionally, an unseen transom divides business and tech programs from humanities programs. A typical humanities graduate will likely never take a coding class and vice versa. I was once speaking to a group of humanities majors about the importance of learning the language of computer code in order to be part of these critical conversations. I realized the irony in the difficulty of trying to convince humanities majors of the importance of learning a new language.

We are starting to see this approach in some universities. The d.school at Stanford seeks to be a space where students can learn human-centered approaches to designing and building practical solutions. The New School, located in New York City, recently launched a new minor called "Code as a Liberal Art," which teaches computer science not as a tool for career preparation, but for creative expression, cultural criticism, and "civic awareness for understanding an increasingly computational society."[14] And Brigham Young University is pioneering an approach it calls Humanities+, in which all humanities majors are encouraged to gain experience in tech or business fields before they graduate, and vice versa. In our future world, it should become increasingly difficult to distinguish between humanities and business or tech programs if we want to create a generation of tech leaders who know how to build virtual spaces with humans at the center. As James Bridle wisely notes, making our online world more human-friendly will not be addressed by building the technology better but by changing the society that is producing these technologies. Universities must realize that they are not just creating software engineers, but the designers of our virtual governments, digital community spaces, and online education institutions.

As parents, we should reach out to schools, universities, and educators to emphasize the urgent need to teach our children to be healthy digital citizens. We should be active collaborators with education partners to keep these issues at the forefront. We should encourage our children to seek out postsecondary education opportunities at institutions that understand the importance of blurring the lines between tech and the humanities, or at least help our children create such programs for themselves by taking a nontraditional blend of courses. We need a generation of designers that understands the priority of building tools that run our virtual world in a way that supports and empowers humanity.

The Missing Team Members

In addition to the members of our digital citizenship team that we've considered, we need to recognize a couple of players that are not yet part of our team in the way they should be. These are groups that can make a unique contribution but have not yet been deeply involved because we have not made digital citizenship a priority for them.

Researchers

More research is necessary to help us understand the best approaches and impact of our work to prepare young people to thrive in a digital world. Sandra Cortesi, a fellow at the Berkman Klein Center for Internet & Society at Harvard University and the director of youth and media, focuses on researching the elements of digital citizenship: which models matter, what skills are being taught, and areas where additional research is needed to understand how young people can become successful in the digital world. But Cortesi's focus is something of an outlier in respect to our national research agenda. The US Department of Education gives around $200 million in funding for education research each year, yet there is no dedicated focus on studying or supporting creating healthy digital citizens. Likewise none of the $60 billion federal defense R&D budget is focused on digital citizenship, even though our greatest national security risk is our own inability to maintain a civil society in a virtual space.[15] If we are serious about the digital well-being of our children, we must also be willing to prioritize an associated national research agenda.

Librarians

We have coaches for music, art, math, sports, just about everything a kid may need. Everything, that is, except for navigating the digital world. Lisa Guernsey, an author and expert on how literacy skills have morphed in the digital world, says all kids need media mentors—nonjudgmental, tech-savvy individuals who can help understand our kids' interests and point them to appropriate media and online experiences. Librarians are uniquely suited to play this role. In many ways, it's the same skill set librarians have used for years to match kids with the right books and provide meaningful context around the ideas they are exploring.

As books themselves increasingly become digital, having large rooms of paper books in every community library is less necessary. Even if you prefer to read a paper book, there are far more efficient ways to store and distribute paper books with the help of virtual apps than having them lined up on a shelf in a physical building. We need the libraries of the future to play a more critical societal function than book storage or internet access points. Imagine if libraries redesigned themselves around being the center for digital learning for our communities? The staff at Providence Public Library in Rhode Island has already begun working digital-citizenship coaching skills into their daily practice. The library offers a Data Navigators 2.0 program that teaches high school students and members of the community basic principles of data analytics and data visualization so they can be informed digital citizens. A Teen Squad program builds on these skills by coaching young people through the use of technology to help solve important problems in collaboration with a variety of local community organizations. The principles of digital citizenship discussed in this book are woven through the library's programs. In a great example of team members working together, the library programs are provided in partnership with the Rhode Island Department of Education so that participating students can get academic credit for what they are learning and, in the summer programs, actually get *paid* for participation as part of a strategic workplace development initiative. As students develop these critical skills they are awarded microcredentials (digital badges) that can help them qualify for future employment and postsecondary education opportunities.[16]

Librarians could become the coaches that our communities need to reinforce digital citizenship skills, particularly when it comes to finding and evaluating the best digital content. Instead of looking to librarians for the distribution of books or providing a space for internet access, we may be better served by seeing librarians as our expert community guides to help navigate and make meaning out of a complex digital world.

Public Media Platforms

Some final missing team members that we should consider are public media platforms. To understand the importance of their role, let's take a minute to look at the history of television. In the 1950s and '60s, there were limited options for high-quality television content for children and a realization that as a society, we should use TV for more aspirational goals. To address the failure of commercial television to provide quality media for children in the United States, Congress passed the Public Broadcasting Act, creating PBS, NPR, *Mr. Roger's Neighborhood*, and *Sesame Street*—all of which were founded on public interest values about what we want kids to learn. Literally every single minute of a PBS Kids show is informed by educational research, reviewed for age appropriateness, and aligned to learning outcomes. Additionally, the fact that these were nonprofit entities allowed them to address important sensitive issues that for-profit companies tended to avoid, like poverty, racism, and stereotyping.

For decades, public media organizations played a staple role in our society, not only making sure quality children's programming was available but also producing news and educational content for adults. But in today's virtual world, we have shifted away from the model where a limited set of organizations produce the media we consume. Now the vast majority of the news and other media is produced by individuals and shared on social media platforms. But to date, there has not been any significant public platform to host these digital media communities. Our main third spaces for sharing digital media—Facebook, YouTube, TikTok, Twitter, Instagram, Reddit, Amazon—are all for-profit companies.

We need public media to evolve to play the same role in our virtual world that it played so effectively for many years in our analog media world. We need virtual community spaces that are free to the public, with the sole purpose of supporting our virtual media-sharing community. By removing the dependence on ad revenue, the design and experience of these community public media spaces could be different. The ways our personal data would be used could be different. And most importantly, a publicly owned version of YouTube or Facebook—with features and functionality that would provide us a noncommercial social gathering place—could actually be a forcing function to improve the experience provided by commercial community platforms. We could easily fund the whole effort through a small tax on targeted online advertising. Without adding public virtual community spaces, our future society depends entirely on commercial entities to permit us to gather and engage as a virtual community.

Being digital for good is a team sport. Families remain at the center of preparing their kids to be effective digital citizens, but they should not be expected to shoulder the burden alone. We should be continually identifying potentially missing members of the team and work in partnership with social platform providers, governments, and educational institutions to create an effective environment for our kids. This means helping these institutions understand what we're expecting, where they are falling short, and what they could be doing differently. If every person who reads this book reaches out to at least one digital platform provider, school, or elected leader to push them to be a more engaged member of the digital citizenship team, there would be a momentum started that would bring about meaningful change and deeper collaboration around a shared goal of preparing our kids to be safe and effective digital citizens.

Next Steps

Action Items

- Reach out to your elected leaders and let them know that they need to take action to ensure adequate protections are in place for our online data.

- Use the feedback tools when problematic posts are made on shared media sites so the platform providers can take action.

- Use feedback channels to ask platform providers to verify user identity and to be transparent about which users are verified.

- Use feedback channels to ask platform providers to more clearly establish and enforce norms of appropriate behavior on their sites.

- Encourage older kids to get experience being moderators in online spaces, including Wikipedia, Reddit, and other online forums.

- Ask school leaders and librarians how they are teaching digital citizenship beyond online safety.

Conversation Starters (for other team members)

- Platform providers:
  - What more could you be doing to verify the identity of the users on your platform?
  - How are you establishing and enforcing norms?

- Government leaders:
  - What policies should be in place to protect our data from being used and shared without our permission?
  - How will you prioritize funding for research and implementation around teaching digital citizenship?
  - How can we ensure universal access to the internet?

- School leaders:
  - How are you teaching students digital citizenship?
  - What is the plan for teaching coding and other digital skills?

9

Our Digital Future

The Greek philosopher Heraclitus once said, "Change is the only constant in life." It's hard to think of any area where that is more applicable than in parenting and technology. It is admittedly hard to discuss the intersection of technology and parenting, knowing that the subject itself is a moving target. Toby Negrin, Wikimedia Foundation's chief product officer, says that the internet is in its adolescence at best. So, as we wind down, let's take a minute to look toward the future of our digital world.

Unanswered (and Evolving) Questions

We will certainly see some interesting technological changes over the next decade. Keyboards will likely become obsolete, as voice recognition continues to improve and we become better at learning how to speak to devices. There will be a continued blur between the virtual and physical worlds. Wearable displays will layer digital information on top of our physical environment, and handheld devices will know when we are in an airport or a grocery store and accordingly provide a different experience. Many much smarter people than I have spent lots of time predicting what the tech of the future will look like (so if you're interested in that, visit *Wired* or *Popular Mechanics*).

To me, the most important elements of the future for us to consider are not the new digital devices, but the ways our digital society will continue to evolve. Instead of making specific predictions, I will frame our look forward by sharing some tough questions that our children will need to be prepared to answer as they grow into leaders of our virtual world. There are, of course, many potential questions, but these four underscore the urgency of providing our kids with a foundation of digital citizenship skills.

Who Should Have Access to Our Data?

As more moments of our lives play out in digital spaces and more data systems become interoperable, our digital footprint can easily provide a complete picture of who we are and what we are doing at all moments of our lives. Digital platform providers and governments alike will be able to gain an increasingly detailed view of all our actions. There are benefits to having detailed and interoperable digital footprints. For one, there is the potential for making the world a safer place. Data trails can help identify people who are using digital tools for fraud and other malicious purposes and warn us of risks before members of our family are harmed by them. Facial-recognition technologies, which are already powerful enough to identify specific individuals in a crowd walking down the street, can be a godsend to help find a family member if they are ever missing or in danger. Facial recognition is already widely used in airports to prevent criminals from illegally entering the country and to speed up immigration lines. Whole cities in China are now deploying similar technology to reduce crime.[1]

But there are also some serious risks to having a digital snapshot of our lives available to governments or private-sector companies. For starters, digital algorithms make mistakes. In 2020, Robert

Julian-Borchak Williams was wrongly arrested for theft when he was mistakenly identified by a facial-recognition algorithm in Detroit.[3] The fact that Williams is a Black man additionally raised questions about whether the algorithms made a mistake or whether the incident was a manifestation of racial bias in the design of the algorithms themselves.

Second, information in our data footprint can outlive its usefulness. Yes, our data trail can help identify someone who may be using the virtual world to scam or harm us, but how long should our digital footprint persist? Is there a point where someone should be forgiven for a past mistake? If your child is flagged for making an inappropriate post on Instagram in junior high, should that be factored into his eligibility score when applying to college or for a job? Should we have the right to audit or remove parts of our digital footprint? Do *we* own our data, or is it the intellectual property of the entities that collect it? What protections need to be in place to make sure our data isn't used to manipulate our political beliefs or exploit our fears and weaknesses for commercial gain? China has received lots of media attention for using citizens' digital data streams as part of a social credit system where law-abiding citizens are rewarded and those who are not behaving appropriately lose privileges. As other countries look to this example, how will we find the line between using our data to keep us safe and creating unauthorized mass surveillance? Deciding who should have access to our data and for what purpose is one of the most important questions we will have to ask as our digital world evolves.

What Do We Do When Truth Becomes Harder to Verify?

A second tough question that our children will face, along with us, is what to do when our current approaches to verify truth can no longer keep up. As discussed in chapter 4, today's digital world is awash in viral misinformation. But for now, the reason is not because the truth is hard to verify as much as the fact that we have not put value in making the effort to do the verifying. What happens in a future digital world where manipulated information becomes nearly impossible to verify using current techniques? Deepfakes, as they are known, are digital media that are so perfectly fabricated they are essentially indistinguishable from real media. They could be a video of a national leader threatening to declare war on another country, a doctor giving a press release about incorrect ways to respond to a pandemic that could actually lead to its spread, or a financial leader making a false report that destabilizes global markets.

We're already beginning to see this happen. Recently, the leader of a British energy company transferred hundreds of thousands of dollars to a bank account at the "request" of the company's CEO. The voice, created using deepfake technology, made the fraudster's voice identical to the voice of the actual CEO.[2] How will we know what to believe when fabricated audio and video are indistinguishable from the real thing? How will we keep from escalating political tensions? Even prior to deepfakes, misinterpreting social media has already come close to causing war. What technologies will be needed to verify the authenticity of a friend or family member before trusting that a call from them is legitimate? Is there an encryption that we should be adding to video or audio files to detect when they have been manipulated? Should there be designated secure platforms for critical national messaging instead of using commercial social media platforms to distribute official communications?

How Should We Pay for Our Virtual Spaces?

In many places throughout this book, we've talked about the challenges caused by the underlying advertising-based business model of our virtual shared spaces. At the current rate, the continual optimization of our shared communities around increasing ad views may eventually destroy the third places that are so critical for a functioning society. In his powerful TED Talk, tech philosopher and father of virtual reality Jaron Lanier states that we cannot have a functioning society in which, if two people wish to communicate, the only way it can happen is if it's financed by a third person who wishes to manipulate them.[4] Companies that serve ads on their site are essentially brokers of eyeballs and clicks. The entities purchasing the ad space determine the content of the ad and are financially driven to optimize that content to get the most-effective results (clicks) for their money. Do we need a fundamentally different way to pay for the internet?

Stefan Thomas, an expert on web monetization, believes that for 15 cents a day, we could remove online advertising from the internet. Thomas believes that by using a browser extension to track the pages we visit, his system could transfer a small payment—maybe just a fraction of a cent—from our digital wallet to the content creator based on our visits. According to Thomas, this would be equivalent to what most sites today receive from ad revenue anyway. And if the $5 per month is more than we're willing to pay for a better web experience, the same technology could support a model in which we earn credits by participating in certain activities (moderating content in a virtual community or reviewing products that we've purchased, etc.) and distributing those credits to the sites we visit. This approach could even allow site creators to develop multiple versions of their site—a basic experience or an enhanced experience for those who choose to share additional credits with the site creator.

Are there other business models we should consider to pay for the sites we use as community spaces? Do we have the right balance between the number of virtual platforms that are publicly owned and those that are commercially owned? Are we willing to pay for virtual experiences that prioritize ensuring civil discourse? Are there ways to incentivize companies to make preserving humanity a core design element?

What Is the Value of Being Human?

Perhaps the most important question that our kids will need to grapple in their digital future is "what value do humans have in a virtual world?" Compared to the three previous questions, this one may sound esoteric, but I mean it very literally. Consider that for hundreds of thousands of years, humans have held a monopoly on essentially every complex skill—speaking, reasoning, problem-solving, engineering, researching. We've never had to question the value of human skills because there was never any competition. However, in a world of artificial intelligence, our unique monopoly no longer exists. AI can already drive safer, provide better customer service, conduct better market analyses, and close retail sales more effectively than humans.

A new company called NEON recently launched a line of artificial humans that can be used to take on a variety of complex tasks. These artificial intelligences are designed to look like and interact like real humans, but they only exist in the virtual world. Each virtual human has specific skill sets; they learn, adapt, and remember what they have learned. Imagine having a Zoom meeting with an architect or an accountant who looks and talks just like any other person you've met on a video call, except they're not human. Whether our children go into careers in music or engineering, accounting or graphic design, they will be working on teams that are not entirely composed of human collaborators. So, in this new world, it is entirely reasonable to ask what value humans bring. Are there uniquely human skills? Are attributes like empathy, humor, creativity, and love our unique value-add? If so, how can this awareness push us to double down on the skills that are particularly human in order to differentiate ourselves from our AI counterparts? Are there certain decisions or actions that should be reserved for humans only?

These four questions are certainly not the only ones that we will need to ask as our virtual world continues to evolve. But they represent the types of issues our children will need to be ready to address as they help us shape the future of our digital democracy.

The Same Principles Still Apply

If you find the challenges of our future online world overwhelming, you're not alone. And I am completely aware that I've had the nerve to present these issues without even proposing clear solutions. I include them merely to make the point that if the next generation is going to be prepared to grapple with the challenges of preserving a functioning digital and physical society, there is urgency to build a foundation of digital citizenship now. The fundamental skills required for answering these and other tough questions are exactly the same ones we've been exploring throughout this book. The principles of becoming digitally balanced, informed, inclusive, engaged, and alert don't just help our kids be happy and healthy now, but create the societal bench strength to address future challenges for years to come.

- By teaching our kids to be *balanced* digital citizens, they will become familiar with the concept that we constantly need to check and monitor our digital habits. It will become second nature to be on the lookout for any digital activities, now and in the future, that start to dominate their lives—and they will have the awareness to make necessary adjustments.

- By teaching our kids to be *informed* digital citizens, they will be prepared with a healthy skepticism for information that shows up in their digital feeds. And they will have the skills to verify and discover answers that go deeper than a simple Google search. Informed digital citizens will create new solutions for spotting deepfakes and validating digital content.

- By teaching our kids to be *inclusive* digital citizens, they will be a force for identifying bias and prejudice that is encoded into our digital world. They will recognize the necessity of varied viewpoints to help them learn and grow.

- By teaching our kids to be *engaged* digital citizens, they will grow up understanding that their devices are also problem-solving tools. While technology creates a number of complex questions that we must ask, it also gives us new ways to provide answers to the challenges. Engaged digital citizens do not just passively accept the world around them but see it as an evolving space for them to build and improve.

- By teaching our kids to be *alert* digital citizens, they will be aware of the monetary and societal value of their personal information, and they will give it the protection it deserves. They will expect digital tools to allow them to control the amount of data they share and with whom. Alert digital citizens will call on tech developers to do more to make sure our shared virtual spaces are safe and will be the creators of new tools to protect their own data as well.

By modeling the five attributes of digital citizenship, we can set our kids up for success now and simultaneously prepare them with the foundational skills they need to lead and shape our digital future.

Final Thoughts

I have three final thoughts that will wrap up our exploration of the roles and responsibilities for teaching digital citizenship.

It's OK to Press Reset

After reading this book, you may feel as though the digital habits or patterns that currently exist in your family are not the ones you should have chosen. Don't beat yourself up. We are the first generation of parents, teachers, and community leaders to raise kids in a ubiquitously digital world. We have to start somewhere. No matter how old your kids are or what patterns and habits they have already formed, it's never too late to reset and improve our efforts around digital well-being.

You don't have to tackle everything at once. The suggested actions at the end of each chapter of this book give over a hundred specific ideas you can implement. Pick one from each chapter that feels most relevant to your unique situation. If there are ideas in this book that don't fit your family goals or style, that's fine. Just pick the elements that feel most aligned and start to work on those. Maybe it's as simple as deciding that phones don't stay in the bedroom at night or turning off autoplay on video services. Perhaps it's getting in the habit of suggesting apps to your kids that align with their interests or having a family challenge to do something every day to spread kindness online.

Teaching digital citizenship in our families is not about creating a checklist but creating a culture. We might draw inspiration from Harvard Business School professor Clayton Christensen's influential book *How Will You Measure Your Life?* He and his coauthors focus on the importance of determining the elements of a family's unique culture and values: Do we value hard work in our family? Do we celebrate serving others in the community? What are the things our family finds funny? What is not to be laughed about? What will we talk openly about and what should be private? Christensen et al. suggest that one of the most important jobs of parents is to explicitly decide what will be part of our family culture and then align our activities to reinforce that culture.

Establishing expectations for the type of digital presence we will have is a critical part of any family's culture. Families should be explicit about creating a culture of using tech for good and not be haphazard about teaching digital citizenship skills.

Parents Have Power

I often hear parents expressing how powerless they feel when they try to control the way devices or social media are negatively impacting their family. Parents have much more power in this situation than they may realize. Especially for young children, parents approve the apps they use and provide them with the devices they use. These are all teachable moments to reinforce ideas of being balanced, alert, and engaged, as we've discussed in this book. And don't underestimate the power of modeling effective behaviors yourself. Your children will pick up on the way you use your devices—and when you choose not to—if you remember to be more overt about it ("I'm turning off my phone because it's time for dinner," "I'm using See Click Fix to report a pothole in the road that needs to be fixed," and so on).

I routinely find parents who forget that they own the internet and data services that their family uses. Sometimes young people buy their own devices, but I don't think I've ever heard of a case where a thirteen-year-old had their own internet service installed in their home. *You* control what comes through the data pipes. If there is digital content you don't feel comfortable having in your home, you can control it through web filters installed on your Wi-Fi network and (for a few extra dollars a month) on cellular data plans as well. While we shouldn't rely only on technical protections, at the same time we should never abdicate one of our easiest and most important parental responsibilities.

Finally, remember that parental voice matters. If there are experiences on digital media platforms that you don't like, or controls you wish existed but don't, say something about it. Just do a quick search for how to provide feedback on any online service or app, and you should be able to quickly find a form or email address to use. Numbers matter, so the more parents and educators who provide similar feedback, the more likely features will be changed. And definitely take more advantage of the existing tools to flag any problematic content you come across online. Parents' voices matter to policy makers as well. If you're concerned that there isn't enough oversight of the amount of advertising that your children see or the use of their data for targeted advertising, say something to your elected representatives. If you feel it's important that your school do more to teach concepts of digital citizenship, share that with your school leaders or school board members.

Parents are not powerless. Through our words and actions, we have much more control over our kids' digital experience than we may realize.

Use Tech on Our Terms

There is a common theme that ties all of the ideas and strategies for digital citizenship together—that in order to maintain digital well-being and create a brighter digital universe, we need to be solidly grounded in the principle of using tech on our terms.

We want our children to know how to always be in control of their digital choices. They should have the agency and strategies to call the shots on their digital experience. If young people have learned digital balance, they are in control of their actions, not ignoring important activities because a single app or game monopolizes their lives. They quickly recognize apps and services that are designed to trick them into giving up their agency by punishing them for not playing more.

If our kids are dealing with the digital world on their own terms, they remain informed; their opinions and ideas are not artificially swayed by bots or ad-driven media that are more concerned about getting clicks than providing them with useful learning experiences. They are remaining alert, not setting themselves up to be bullied or coerced into activities that they do not want to participate in. Apps and virtual platforms may be designed to limit their agency, but digital citizens who know how to use technology on their own terms see through these traps and adjust settings or engage in different online activities entirely so they remain in control.

Kids who learn to engage in the virtual world on their own terms view the standards of their family's digital culture as nonnegotiables. They become increasingly independent and responsible over time; not making decisions because their parents are forcing them but because they understand the value behind being a force for good online and have practiced the associated behaviors for years.

Two Possible Futures

One of my favorite nineties movies is *Sliding Doors*. Set in London, the movie begins with Helen (Gwyneth Paltrow) losing her public relations job and heading home in the middle of the day. She enters the Underground station and runs toward her train, barely catching it before it pulls away from the platform. A few minutes later, the exact same scene repeats itself; only this time as she's running toward the train, a child bumps into her, causing her to stop for a second.

The delay causes her to miss the train, and she's left standing on the platform. From there, the movie continues switching back and forth between her two possible futures: the one where she catches the train and the one where she misses it. Over the course of the movie, we see Helen's life end up in two unimaginably different places, just based on having missed that train. This movie has always fascinated me, perhaps because I've spent much of my life barely missing various forms of public transportation. But also because I can't help pondering the warning of how much a single decision can shape our future.

As we consider the digital world that our kids will grow up in, we are at a point where we have to choose between two very distinct, possible futures. In one possible future, we continue on our current path. We remain haphazard in our approach to preparing kids for success online, emphasizing the don'ts and focusing only on the basics of safety without exploring other critical attributes of digital well-being. We become increasingly resigned to the reality that our kids will grow up in a virtual world that has the primary goal of stealing their data and providing misinformation to generate more ad revenue. We sit back and watch as the algorithms of the digital world reinforce their current beliefs and insulate them into comfort bubbles. The division seeded by the sense of artificial rightness that we all feel when digital media reinforces our beliefs, whatever they are and however wrong they may be, will relentlessly continue to tear apart the fabric of our society.

But, then, there is another future—a brighter future. One where we decide to be deliberate and thoughtful about preparing our kids for success in the digital world. Where we recognize that teaching digital citizenship is much more than online safety, but helping our kids use the virtual world to enhance their lives and improve their communities. We focus on a positive approach, teaching the dos—the skills they can practice to become effective digital citizens. We teach them to find balance between their various online and offline activities. We hold online platform providers to an expectation that they must design their tools in a way that supports humanity and democracy. And we expect governments to play an active role in ensuring a just and sustainable virtual world that prioritizes supporting civility over profits. In this future, technology strengthens our families and helps accelerate problem-solving to improve our local and global communities.

We can choose which future we want. As the migration to our digital world accelerates through new advances in technologies, we have a limited window in which to make the decision before the train will have left the station. I'm optimistic for our future. I believe that technology will make us better people by supporting and supercharging the best of our human abilities. But technology has no conscience— that's our job. The same technologies that can solve our toughest human problems can also divide and destroy us with a remarkable efficiency.

The digital world is now our primary residence. That will not change. But how we shape our digital future remains entirely in our hands and the hands of our children. Our children will always be digital. Let's make sure they are also digital for good.

NOTES

Introduction

1. International Workplace Group, "The IWG Global Workspace Survey," March 2019, https://assets.regus.com/pdfs/iwg-workplace-survey/iwg-workplace-survey -2019.pdf.

2. Andrei Zimiles, "Four New Statistics That Prove That Telemedicine Isn't Just a Pandemic Fad," Medical Economics, July 8, 2020, https://www.medicaleconomics.com /view/four-new-statistics-that-prove-that-telemedicine-isn-t-just-a-pandemic-fad.

3. Tugba Sabanoglu, "Number of Digital Buyers in the United States from 2017 to 2024," Statista, November 30, 2020, https://www.statista.com/statistics/273957/number -of-digital-buyers-in-the-united-states/; Shopify, "The Future of Ecommerce in 2021," 2021, https://www.shopify.com/enterprise/the-future-of-ecommerce.

4. Alex Shashkevich, "Meeting Online Has Become the Most Popular Way U.S. Couples Connect, Stanford Sociologist Finds," *Stanford News*, August 21, 2019, https:// news.stanford.edu/2019/08/21/online-dating-popular-way-u-s-couples-meet/.

5. Katherine Timpf, "OKCupid Allowing Users to Identify as Five Sexual Orienta-tions at Once," *National Review*, November 18, 2014, https://www.nationalreview.com /2014/11/okcupid-allowing-users-identify-five-sexual-orientations-once-katherine -timpf/.

6. Doug Lederman, "Online Education Ascends," *Inside Higher Ed*, November 7, 2018, https://www.insidehighered.com/digital-learning/article/2018/11/07/new-data -online-enrollments-grow-and-share-overall-enrollment.

7. YouTube Internal Data, Global, 2017, https://www.thinkwithgoogle.com /marketing-strategies/video/learning-related-youtube-statistics/.

8. Roger Vincent, "That Canter's Pastrami Takeout You Ordered Might Be Com-ing from a Ghost Kitchen," *Los Angeles Times*, January 30, 2020, https://www.latimes.com /business/story/2020-01-30/that-canters-pastrami-takeout-you-ordered-might-be-coming -from-a-ghost-kitchen.

9. Miles Parks, "Exclusive: Seattle-Area Voters to Vote by Smartphone in 1st for U.S. Election," NPR, January 22, 2020, https://www.npr.org/2020/01/22/798126153 /exclusive-seattle-area-voters-to-vote-by-smartphone-in-1st-for-u-s-elections.

10. Graham Kendall, "Apollo 11 Anniversary: Could an iPhone Fly Me to the Moon?" *Independent*, July 9, 2019, https://www.independent.co.uk/news/science/apollo -11-moon-landing-mobile-phones-smartphone-iphone-a8988351.html.

11. Nick Bilton, "Steve Jobs Was a Low-Tech Parent," *New York Times*, September 10, 2014, https://www.nytimes.com/2014/09/11/fashion/steve-jobs-apple-was-a-low-tech -parent.html?_r=0.

Chapter 1

1. Flight Safety Australia, "178 Seconds to Live—VFR into IMC," January 22, 2016, https://www.flightsafetyaustralia.com/2016/01/178-seconds-to-live-vfr-into-imc/.

2. Committee on Communications, "Children, Adolescents, and Advertising," *Pediatrics* 118, no. 6 (2006): 2563–2569.

3. Lisa Guernsey, *Screen Time*, Kindle ed. (New York: Basic Books, 2012), 223.

4. Keith Wagstaff, "How Target Knew a High School Girl Was Pregnant before Her Parents Did," *Time*, February 17, 2012, techland.time.com/2012/02/17/how-target-knew-a-high-school-girl-was-pregnant-before-her-parents/.

5. Centers for Disease Control and Prevention, "E-Cigarette Ads and Youth," https://www.cdc.gov/vitalsigns/ecigarette-ads/index.html.

6. Guernsey, *Screen Time*, 225.

7. Naomi Kresge, Ilya Khrennikov, and David Ramli, "Period-Tracking Apps Are Monetizing Women's Extremely Personal Data," *Bloomberg Businessweek*, January 24, 2019, https://www.bloomberg.com/news/articles/2019-01-24/how-period-tracking-apps-are-monetizing-women-s-extremely-personal-data.

8. Zeynep Tufekci, "We're Building a Dystopia Just to Make People Click on Ads," TED Talk, September 2017, https://www.ted.com/talks/zeynep_tufekci_we_re_building_a_dystopia_just_to_make_people_click_on_ads.

9. Amanda Todd Legacy Society, "About Amanda, Amanda's Story," https://www.amandatoddlegacy.org/about-amanda.html.

10. Monisha Martins, "Predators Lurk Behind Computer Screens," *Maple Ridge-Pitt Meadows News*, October 25, 2012, https://www.mapleridgenews.com/news/predators-lurk-behind-computer-screens/.

11. TheSomebodytoKnow, "My Story: Struggling, Bullying, Suicide, Self Harm," YouTube video, September 7, 2012, https://www.youtube.com/watch?v=vOHXGNx-E7E.

12. Monica Anderson, "A Majority of Teens Have Experienced Some Form of Cyberbullying," Pew Research Center, September 27, 2018, https://www.pewresearch.org/internet/2018/09/27/a-majority-of-teens-have-experienced-some-form-of-cyberbullying/.

13. Young Minds, "Safety Net Report: Impact of Cyberbullying on Children's Mental Health," https://youngminds.org.uk/resources/policy-reports/cyberbullying-inquiry/; McAfee, "Teens' Online Behavior Can Get Them in Trouble," June 3, 2014, https://www.mcafee.com/blogs/consumer/family-safety/teens-and-screens/.

14. Jessica Guynn, "If You've Been Harassed Online, You're Not Alone: More Than Half of Americans Say They've Experienced Hate," *USA Today*, February 13, 2019, https://www.usatoday.com/story/news/2019/02/13/study-most-americans-have-been-targeted-hateful-speech-online/2846987002/; J. Clement, "Percentage of Teenagers in the United States Who Have Encountered Hate Speech on Social Media Platforms as of April 2018, by Type," Statista, October 14, 2019, https://www.statista.com/statistics/945392/teenagers-who-encounter-hate-speech-online-social-media-usa/.

15. Becky Gardiner et al., "The Dark Side of Guardian Comments," *Guardian*, April 12, 2016, https://www.theguardian.com/technology/2016/apr/12/the-dark-side-of-guardian-comments.

16. Sherri Gordon, "How the Bullying Tactics Politicians Use Affect Kids," Verywell Family, June 21, 2020, https://www.verywellfamily.com/5-bullying-tactics-politicians-use-and-how-it-impacts-kids-4080749.

17. Rebecca Webber, "The Comparison Trap," *Psychology Today*, November 2017, https://www.psychologytoday.com/us/articles/201711/the-comparison-trap.

18. Seth Stephens-Davidowitz, "Don't Let Facebook Make You Miserable," *New York Times*, May 6, 2017, https://www.nytimes.com/2017/05/06/opinion/sunday/dont-let-facebook -make-you-miserable.html.

19. Jacqueline Nesi and Mitchell J. Prinstein, "Using Social Media for Social Comparison and Feedback-Seeking: Gender and Popularity Moderate Associations with Depressive Symptoms," *Journal of Abnormal Child Psychology* 43, no. 8 (2015): 1427–1438.

20. Jasmine Garsd, "#Blessed: Is Everyone Happier Than You on Social Media?," NPR, August 6, 2018, https://www.npr.org/2018/08/06/636016812/-blessed-is-everyone -happier-than-you-on-social-media.

21. Royal Society for Public Health, "#StatusofMind," https://www.rsph.org.uk /our-work/campaigns/status-of-mind.html.

22. Samantha Cole, "The Ugly Truth Behind Pornhub's 'Year in Review'," Vice, February 18, 2020, https://www.vice.com/en/article/wxez8y/pornhub-year-in-review -deepfake.

23. Fight the New Drug, "How Consuming Porn Can Lead to Violence," August 23, 2017, https://fightthenewdrug.org/how-consuming-porn-can-lead-to-violence/; Revealing Reality,"Young People, Pornography, and Age-Verification," BBFC report, https:// www.revealingreality.co.uk/work/young-people-pornography-age-verification/.

24. Eli Saslow, "'Nothing on This Page Is Real': How Lies Become Truth in Online America," *Washington Post*, November 17, 2018, https://www.washingtonpost.com /national/nothing-on-this-page-is-real-how-lies-become-truth-in-online-america/2018 /11/17/edd44cc8-e85a-11e8-bbdb-72fdbf9d4fed_story.html; Craig Silverman, Jane Lytvynenko, and Scott Pham, "These Are 50 of the Biggest Fake News Hits on Facebook in 2017," BuzzFeed News, December 28, 2017, https://www.buzzfeednews .com/article/craigsilverman/these-are-50-of-the-biggest-fake-news-hits-on-facebook -in#.xtG2LmjYnN.

25. BBC News, "Coronavirus: How a Misleading Map Went Global," February 19, 2020, https://www.bbc.com/news/world-51504512.

26. Knight Foundation, "Disinformation, 'Fake News' and Influence Campaigns on Twitter," October 4, 2018, https://knightfoundation.org/reports/disinformation-fake -news-and-influence-campaigns-on-twitter/.

27. Amy Watson, "Share of Adults Who Believe Fake News Is a Major Problem in the United States in 2017, by Age," Statista, December 12, 2019, https://www.statista .com/statistics/657061/fake-news-confusion-level-by-age/; Statista, "Fake News in Europe—Statistics and Facts," June 5, 2020, https://www.statista.com/topics/5833/fake -news-in-europe/.

28. US House of Representatives Permanent Select Committee on Intelligence, "Exposing Russia's Effort to Sow Discord Online: The Internet Research Agency and Advertisements," https://intelligence.house.gov/social-media-content/.

29. Franklin Foer, "Putin Is Well on His Way to Stealing the Next Election," *Atlantic*, June 2020, https://www.theatlantic.com/magazine/archive/2020/06/putin-american -democracy/610570/.

30. Scott Shane and Vindu Goel, "Fake Russian Facebook Accounts Bought $100,000 in Political Ads," *New York Times*, September 6, 2017, https://www.nytimes.com/2017/09/06 /technology/facebook-russian-political-ads.html.

31. Philip N. Howard, Bharath Ganesh, and Dimitra Liotsiou, "The IRA, Social Media and Political Polarization in the United States, 2012-2018," Oxford University,

Computational Propaganda Research Project, https://comprop.oii.ox.ac.uk/wp-content/uploads/sites/93/2018/12/IRA-Report.pdf.

32. David Von Drehle, "Vladimir Putin's Virus," *Washington Post*, March 2, 2020, https://www.washingtonpost.com/opinions/2020/03/02/did-vladimir-putin-turn-america-itself/.

33. Jonathan Haidt and Tobias Rose-Stockwell, "The Dark Psychology of Social Networks," *Atlantic*, December 2019, https://www.theatlantic.com/magazine/archive/2019/12/social-media-democracy/600763/.

34. Scott Galloway, *The Four: The Hidden DNA of Amazon, Apple, Facebook, and Google* (New York: Random House, 2017).

35. McAfee, "The Economic Impact of Cybercrime—No Slowing Down," accessed October 24, 2018.

36. James Bridle, "The Nightmare Videos of Children's YouTube—and What's Wrong with the Internet Today," TED Talk, April 2018, https://www.ted.com/talks/james_bridle_the_nightmare_videos_of_children_s_youtube_and_what_s_wrong_with_the_internet_today?language=en.

Chapter 2

1. Ray Oldenburg, *The Great Good Place: Cafes, Coffee Shops, Community Centers, Beauty Parlors, General Stores, Bars, Hangouts, and How They Get You Through the Day* (New York: Paragon House, 1989).

2. D. L. Cooperrider and S. Srivastva, "Appreciative Inquiry in Organizational Life," in *Research in Organizational Change and Development*, vol. 1, eds. R. W. Woodman and W. A. Pasmore (Stamford, CT: JAI Press, 1987), 129–169.

3. US Department of Education, National Education Technology Plan 2016, "Future Ready Learning: Reimaging the Role of Technology in Education," https://tech.ed.gov/files/2015/12/NETP16.pdf.

4. Tim Omarzu, "Chattanooga STEM Students Control Microscote 1,800 Miles away from L.A.," *Chattanooga Times Free Press*, May 15, 2015, https://www.timesfreepress.com/news/local/story/2015/may/15/stem-school-chattanoogastudents-control-micro/304383/.

Chapter 3

1. Angeline Lillard and Jennifer Peterson, "The Immediate Impact of Different Types of Television on Young Children's Executive Function," *Pediatrics* 128 (2011): 644–649.

2. American Academy of Pediatrics, news release, https://services.aap.org/en/news-room/news-releases/aap/2016/aap-announces-new-recommendations-for-media-use/.

3. US Department of Education, "Early Learning and Educational Technology Policy Brief," October 2016, https://tech.ed.gov/files/2016/10/Early-Learning-Tech-Policy-Brief.pdf.

4. World Health Organization, "Guidelines on Physical Activity, Sedentary Behaviour, and Sleep," https://apps.who.int/iris/bitstream/handle/10665/325147/WHO-NMH-PND-2019.4-eng.pdf.

5. US Department of Education, National Education Technology Plan 2016, "Future Ready Learning: Reimaging the Role of Technology in Education," https://tech.ed.gov/files/2015/12/NETP16.pdf.

6. Thomas H. Davenport and John C. Beck, *The Attention Economy: Understanding the New Currency of Business* (Boston: Harvard Business School Press, 2002).

7. Shalini Paruthi et al., "Recommended Amount of Sleep for Pediatric Populations: A Consensus Statement of the American Academy of Sleep Medicine," *Journal of Clinical Sleep Medicine* 12, no. 6 (2016): 785–786; Eric Suni, "How Much Sleep Do We Really Need?," SleepFoundation.org, July 31, 2020, https://www.sleepfoundation .org/how-sleep-works/how-much-sleep-do-we-really-need.

8. Katherine T. Baum et al., "Sleep Restriction Worsens Mood and Emotion Regulation in Adolescents," *Journal of Child Psychology and Psychiatry* 55, no. 2 (2014): 180–190; Nicole Lovato and Michael Gradisar, "A Meta-Analysis and Model of the Relationship between Sleep and Depression in Adolescents: Recommendations for Future Research and Clinical Practice," *Sleep Medicines Review* 18, no. 6 (2014): 521–529; Lauren Hale et al., "Youth Screen Media Habits and Sleep: Sleep-Friendly Screen-Behavior Recommendations for Clinicians, Educators, and Parents," *Child Adolescent Psychiatry Clinics of North America* 27, no. 2 (2018): 229–245.

9. A. M. Williamson and Anne-Marie Feyer, "Moderate Sleep Deprivation Produces Impairments in Cognitive and Motor Performance Equivalent to Legally Prescribed Levels of Alcohol Intoxication," *Occupational and Environmental Medicine* 57 (2000): 649–655; Lissette Calveiro, "Studies Show Sleep Deprivation Performance Is Similar to Being under the Influence of Alcohol," *HuffPost*, March 31, 2016, https://www.huffpost .com/entry/studies-show-sleep-deprivation-performance-is-similar-to-being-under-the -influence-of-alcohol_b_9562992.

10. Angelina Maric et al., "Insufficient Sleep: Enhanced Risk-Seeking Relates to Low Local Sleep Intensity," *Annals of Neurology* 82, no. 3 (2017): 409–418.

11. Health Sleep, "Sleep, Learning, and Memory," http://healthysleep.med.harvard .edu/healthy/matters/benefits-of-sleep/learning-memory.

12. Hale et al., "Youth Screen Media Habits and Sleep."

13. National Sleep Foundation, "Three Ways Gadgets Are Keeping You Awake," https://www.sleep.org/ways-technology-affects-sleep/.

14. Sydney Johnson, "Almost a Third of Teenagers Sleep with Phones, Survey Finds," EdSource, May 28, 2019, https://edsource.org/2019/almost-a-third-of-teenagers -sleep-with-their-phones-survey-finds/612995.

15. Rina Raphael, "Netflix CEO Reed Hastings: Sleep Is Our Competition," *Fast Company*, November 6, 2017, https://www.fastcompany.com/40491939/netflix-ceo-reed -hastings-sleep-is-our-competition.

16. Natasha Frost, "Mark Zuckerberg Built Priscilla Chan a Screen-Free Bedside Alarm," *Quartz*, April 28, 2019, https://qz.com/1606848/mark-zuckerberg-built-priscilla -chan-a-screen-free-bedside-alarm/.

17. Participatory Learning Leadership and Policy, "Rethinking Acceptable Use Policies to Enable Digital Learning: A Guide for School Districts," revised March 2013, https://www.cosn.org/sites/default/files/pdf/Revised%20AUP%20March%202013_final .pdf.

18. Renton School District, "Responsible Use Policy," https://www.rentonschools .us/learning-and-teaching/digital-learning/responsible-use-policy; Champlain Valley School District, "Technology Use Guidelines for Students," https://docs.google.com /document/d/1A9jyIDk-LL7Ltk_2kThwutMgfNECQOtfttOhaECkn-c/edit.

19. Participatory Learning Leadership and Policy, "Rethinking Acceptable Use Policies to Enable Digital Learning: A Guide for School Districts."

Chapter 4

1. Jacob Soll, "The Long and Brutal History of Fake News," *Politico Magazine*, December 18, 2016, https://www.politico.com/magazine/story/2016/12/fake-news-history-long-violent-214535.

2. Angela Moon, "Two-Thirds of American Adults Get News from Social Media: Survey," Reuters, September 8, 2017, https://www.reuters.com/article/us-usa-internet-socialmedia/two-thirds-of-american-adults-get-news-from-social-media-survey-idUSKCN1BJ2A8.

3. Soroush Vosoughi, Deb Roy, and Sinan Aral, "The Spread of False News Online," *Science* 359, no. 6380 (2018): 1146–1151.

4. Craig Silverman, "This Analysis Shows How Viral Fake Election News Stories Outperformed Real News on Facebook," BuzzFeed News, November 16, 2016, https://www.buzzfeednews.com/article/craigsilverman/viral-fake-election-news-outperformed-real-news-on-facebook.

5. Sheera Frenkel, "Facebook to End News Feed Experiment in 6 Countries That Magnified Fake News," *New York Times*, March 1, 2018, https://www.nytimes.com/2018/03/01/technology/facebook-end-news-feed-experiment-six-countries-that-magnified-fake-news.html.

6. D. J. Leu et al., "Defining Online Reading Comprehension: Using Think Aloud Verbal Protocols to Refine a Preliminary Model of Internet Reading Comprehension Processes" (Annual Meeting of the American Educational Research Association, Chicago, IL, April 9, 2007).

7. Jenny Anderson, "Only 9% of 15-Year-Olds Can Tell the Difference between Fact and Opinion," *Quartz*, December 3, 2019, https://qz.com/1759474/only-9-percent-of-15-year-olds-can-distinguish-between-fact-and-opinion/.

8. Brooke Donald, "Stanford Researchers Find Students Have Trouble Judging the Credibility of Information Online," Stanford Graduate School of Education, November 22, 2016, https://ed.stanford.edu/news/stanford-researchers-find-students-have-trouble-judging-credibility-information-online.

9. Dan Kopf, "Want to Save Democracy? Try Teaching Kids to Read Charts," *Quartz*, January 6, 2019, https://qz.com/1307848/people-dont-understand-how-to-read-charts-fixing-it-starts-with-kids/.

10. Mihai Andrei, "Study Shows Wikipedia Accuracy Is 99.5%," ZME Science, February 22, 2019, https://www.zmescience.com/science/study-wikipedia-25092014/.

11. Todd Rose, *The End of Average: How We Succeed in a World That Values Sameness* (New York: HarperOne, 2016).

Chapter 5

1. David DiSalvo, *What Makes Your Brain Happy and Why You Should Do the Opposite* (Buffalo, NY: Prometheus, 2011).

2. Robert Burton, *On Being Certain: Believing You Are Right Even When You're Not* (New York: St. Martin's Griffin, 2009).

3. Project Implicit, https://implicit.harvard.edu/.

4. Zeynep Tufekci, "YouTube, the Great Radicalizer," *New York Times*, March 10, 2018, https://www.nytimes.com/2018/03/10/opinion/sunday/youtube-politics-radical.html.

5. Sanah Jivani quotes from an interview with author, February 13, 2020.

6. Pew Research Center, "Teens, Kindness, and Cruelty on Social Network Sites," November 9, 2011, https://www.pewresearch.org/internet/2011/11/09/teens-kindness -and-cruelty-on-social-network-sites-2/.

7. Sharon Padgett and Charles E. Notar, "Bystanders Are the Key to Stopping Bullying," *Universal Journal of Educational Research* 1, no. 2 (2013): 33–41.

8. Amanda Scherker, "When This Girl Was Bullied over Her Prom Dress, Her Entire Community Stood up for Her," *HuffPost*, January 13, 2015, https://www.huffpost .com/entry/girl-prom-dress-bullied_n_6462806.

Chapter 6

1. Richard Paul Evans, *The Spyglass: A Book About Faith* (New York: Aladdin, 2014).

2. Jonah Engel Bromwich, "How the Parkland Students Got So Good at Social Media," *New York Times*, March 7, 2018, https://www.nytimes.com/2018/03/07/us /parkland-students-social-media.html.

3. Joseph South, "Civic Engagement Goes Viral When Young Voices Turn to Social Media," Medium, July 20, 2018, https://medium.com/office-of-citizen/civic-engagement -goes-viral-when-young-voices-turn-to-social-media-ea57ed0c5d65.

4. Simon Owens, "How Change.org Is Mastering the Science of Micro-Activism," *U.S. News and World Report*, September 7, 2012, https://www.usnews.com/news/articles /2012/09/07/how-changeorg-is-mastering-the-science-of-micro-activism.

5. School Retool, https://schoolretool.org/.

6. See "P1, Mrs. Jalland, and Ellie Elephant," Twitter, https://twitter.com /ellieprimary1.

7. See "Teaching Global Citizenship Using Social Media and an Elephant—The Videos," Microsoft Sway, https://sway.office.com/Rh3QGqWio3PHfZzJ.

8. Westquarter Primary, "Twin a Toilet," YouTube video, December 5, 2017, https:// www.youtube.com/watch?time_continue=1&v=6NvRljCkLSQ.

9. Stats from "Be My Eyes," https://www.BeMyEyes.com.

10. National Human Trafficking Hotline, "The Victims," https://humantrafficking hotline.org/what-human-trafficking/human-trafficking/victims.

11. TraffickCam, https://traffickcam.com/about.

12. Cancer Research UK, "Protein Folding Becomes Cancer Treatment Target," Medical Xpress, December 3, 2013, https://medicalxpress.com/news/2013-12-protein -cancer-treatment.html.

13. Firas Khatib et al., "Crystal Structure of a Monomeric Retroviral Protease Solved by Protein Folding Game Players," *Nature Structural Molecular Biology* 18, no 10. (2011): 1175–1177.

14. Turner and Graham quotes from an interview with the author, 2019.

15. Sue Shellenbarger, "The Secret Benefits of Retelling Family Stories," *Wall Street Journal*, November 11, 2019, https://www.wsj.com/articles/the-secret-benefits-of -retelling-family-stories-11573468201.

16. Robin Fivush, "Collective Stories in Families Teach Us about Ourselves," *Psychology Today*, February 2, 2017, https://www.psychologytoday.com/us/blog/the -stories-our-lives/201702/collective-stories-in-families-teach-us-about-ourselves.

17. John Roach, "17-Year-Old Girl Builds Artificial 'Brain' to Detect Breast Cancer," NBC News, July 24, 2012, https://www.nbcnews.com/technology/17-year-old-girl-builds -artificial-brain-detect-breast-cancer-908308.

18. Ipsita Basu, "Two Teenagers Developed an App That Links Volunteers and Non-Profit Organisations," *Economic Times*, December 11, 2017, https://economictimes .indiatimes.com/magazines/panache/two-teenagers-developed-an-app-that-links -volunteers-and-non-profit-organisations/articleshow/62018585.cms.

19. Snow Day Calculator, https://www.snowdaycalculator.com/about.php?open =true&.

20. Code for America, "National Day of Civic Hacking 2019," https://www .codeforamerica.org/events/national-day-of-civic-hacking-2019.

Chapter 7

1. Office of Nuclear Energy, "Advantages and Challenges of Nuclear Energy," February 4, 20202, https://www.energy.gov/ne/articles/advantages-and-challenges -nuclear-energy.

2. Nick Huss, "How Many Websites Are There Around the World (2020)?" Siteefy, November 20, 2020, https://www.millforbusiness.com/how-many-websites-are-there/.

3. Scott Galloway, *The Four: The Hidden DNA of Amazon, Apple, Facebook, and Google* (New York: Random House, 2017).

4. Anti-Defamation League, "Cyberbullying Warning Signs," https://www.adl.org /resources/tools-and-strategies/cyberbullying-warning-signs.

Chapter 8

1. Flickr Community guidelines, https://www.flickr.com/help/guidelines/.

2. Jay Hathaway, "This Twitter Bot Tricks Angry Trolls into Arguing with It for Hours," Daily Dot, February 28, 2020, https://www.dailydot.com/unclick/arguebot -twitter-bot-bait-jerks/.

3. Bobby Allyn, "Researchers: Nearly Half of Accounts Tweeting about Coronavirus Are Likely Bots," NPR, May 20, 2020, https://www.npr.org/sections/coronavirus-live -updates/2020/05/20/859814085/researchers-nearly-half-of-accounts-tweeting-about -coronavirus-are-likely-bots; Zoey Chong, "Up to 48 Million Twitter Accounts Are Bots, Study Says," CNET, March 14, 2017, https://www.cnet.com/news/new-study-says-almost -15-percent-of-twitter-accounts-are-bots/.

4. Michael H. Keller, "The Flourishing Business of Fake YouTube Views," *New York Times*, August 11, 2018, https://www.nytimes.com/interactive/2018/08/11/technology /youtube-fake-view-sellers.html.

5. Emily Stewart, "Facebook Has Taken Down Billions of Fake Accounts, But the Problem Is Still Getting Worse," Vox, May 23, 2019, https://www.vox.com/recode /2019/5/23/18637596/facebook-fake-accounts-transparency-mark-zuckerberg-report.

6. Aarti Shahani, "Twitter Adds Warning Label for Offensive Political Tweets," NPR, June 27, 2019, https://www.npr.org/2019/06/27/736668003/twitter-adds-warning -label-for-offensive-political-tweets.

7. Ryan Mac and John Paczkowski, "Apple Has Threatened to Ban Parler from the App Store," BuzzFeed News, January 8, 2021, https://www.buzzfeednews.com/article /ryanmac/apple-threatens-ban-parler.

8. Adam Satariano, "'This Is a New Phase': Europe Shifts Tactics to Limit Tech's Power," *New York Times*, July 30, 2020, https://www.nytimes.com/2020/07/30/technology /europe-new-phase-tech-amazon-apple-facebook-google.html.

9. Committee on Communications, "Children, Adolescents, and Advertising," *Pediatrics* 118, no. 6 (2006): 2563–2569.

10. Wafa Ben-Hassine, "Government Policy for the Internet Must Be Rights-Based and User-Centred," *UN Chronicle*, accessed January 14, 2021, https://www.un.org/en /chronicle/article/government-policy-internet-must-be-rights-based-and-user-centred.

11. Jaron Lanier and E. Glen Weyl, "A Blueprint for a Better Digital Society," HBR .org, September 26, 2018, https://hbr.org/2018/09/a-blueprint-for-a-better-digital-society.

12. Calling Bullshit syllabus, see https://www.callingbullshit.org/syllabus.html.

13. Peter Kelley, "After Much Media Attention, UW Information School's 'Calling BS' Class Begins," UW News, March 28, 2017, https://www.washington.edu/news/2017 /03/28/after-much-media-attention-uw-information-schools-calling-bs-class-begins/.

14. Rebecca Koenig, "Meet the Newest Liberal Art: Coding," EdSurge, February 5, 2020, https://www.edsurge.com/news/2020-02-05-meet-the-newest-liberal-art-coding.

15. Congressional Research Service, "Federal Research and Development (R&D) Funding: FY2020," updated March 18, 2020, https://fas.org/sgp/crs/misc/R45715.pdf.

16. Providence Public Library, "Teen Squad," https://www.provlib.org/education /teen-squad/.

Chapter 9

1. Emily Feng, "How China Is Using Facial Recognition Technology," NPR, December 16, 2019, https://www.npr.org/2019/12/16/788597818/how-china-is-using -facial-recognition-technology.

2. Kashmir Hill, "Wrongfully Accused by an Algorithm," *New York Times*, June 24, 2020, https://www.nytimes.com/2020/06/24/technology/facial-recognition-arrest.html.

3. Catherine Stupp, "Fraudsters Used AI to Mimic CEO's Voice in Unusual Cybercrime Case," *Wall Street Journal*, August 30, 2019, https://www.wsj.com/articles /fraudsters-use-ai-to-mimic-ceos-voice-in-unusual-cybercrime-case-11567157402.

4. Jaron Lanier, "How We Need to Remake the Internet," TED Talk, April 2018, https://www.ted.com/talks/jaron_lanier_how_we_need_to_remake_the_internet ?language=en.

INDEX

ACKNOWLEDGMENTS

The ideas and concepts shared in this book are the result of decades of working with kids, parents, technology innovators, and education experts. In other words, if you found any of the ideas in this book helpful, the credit should be spread among those who were generous enough to share their experiences with me and, in so doing, shaped my thinking. I am blessed to have had Arne Duncan, Elliott Masie, Jonathan Kayes, David Egbert, Al Merkley, Beth Noveck, Dana Karp, Paul Allen, and James Baird as the best team of mentors and life coaches anyone could ever hope for.

When it comes to the topic of digital citizenship, I am particularly appreciative of the insights and inspiration I got from Erik Martin, Eli Pariser, Renee Hobbs, Emily Davis, Jaron Lanier, Zeynep Tufekci, Marina Nitze, and Lisa Guernsey. Their tireless efforts are helping create a better digital world for all of us.

The process of writing a book requires a whole other set of gratitudes. I'm grateful for the encouragement I received from Sandy Speicher, Willa Perlman, and Manoush Zomorodi, who believed in the idea of this book even before I did and whose vote of confidence helped make it a reality. And I can't say enough about the incredible team at Harvard Business Review Press, especially Courtney Cashman, who patiently helped turn my ideas into concepts others could understand, and Jane Gebhart, whose discerning eye and meticulous copyediting made those concepts readable (while also reminding me how little I know about the proper use of semicolons).

I'm grateful to Tiana Page, Mollie Kavanaugh, Brittany Singleton, and the amazing team of innovators at the International Society for

Technology in Education (ISTE) for always pushing my thinking and asking the important questions; to Janna Patterson for helping find data and examples to support the ideas in this book while always making sure the most important voices stayed at the forefront of the conversation; and to Joseph South—whose thoughtful persistence nudges the whole world to a better place—for his unique ability to turn my mediocre ideas into good ones.

I am deeply thankful for my parents: For my dad, Rich Culatta, who in addition to being an indispensable thought partner on this book, by having the same name as me has always made my Google search results look *way* more impressive than they otherwise would be. For my mom, Barbara Culatta, who always encouraged my curiosity and broadened my view of the world. For Jan Culatta, who taught me tenacity and confidence. And for Melinda Baird for being my sounding board and friend.

Finally, I'm incredibly grateful for my family. My wife, Shaundra, patiently endured abandonment and neglect while trying to coach our four kids through online learning as I hid in the closet to write this book. Shaundra is the genius behind many of the ideas presented here and has graciously allowed me to spend more time writing about them than helping her implement them. And to my four amazing kiddos—the willing guinea pigs for my crazy ideas—who take so seriously their responsibility to make the world a better place. Thanks for taking after your mother. Oh, and to Bailey for chewing on my fingers while I was supposed to be writing.

ABOUT THE AUTHOR

RICHARD CULATTA is an internationally recognized learning innovator and tech strategist. His work centers around using technology to empower people and accelerate problem-solving. He is the CEO of the International Society for Technology in Education (ISTE), a nonprofit organization that supports education leaders in 127 countries. Culatta served as the first Chief Innovation Officer for his home state of Rhode Island, where he gained national attention for designing nontraditional approaches that helped government be more responsive to citizen needs.

Culatta was appointed by President Obama as the Executive Director of the Office of Educational Technology for the US Department of Education and was charged with developing a plan to transform US schools through technology. In that capacity, he focused on expanding internet connectivity to schools across the country, promoting personalized learning, and developing a national ed tech plan to close long-standing equity gaps. He also pioneered new opportunities for the tech industry to engage with the Department of Education to address tough problems, including bringing top game designers from around the world to the White House to help redesign testing and learning materials.

Culatta holds degrees in the humanities and in instructional technology from Brigham Young University. He serves as a senior fellow at NYU's GovLab and as a design resident for the global innovation and design firm IDEO. He is married to the violinist Shaundra Baird Culatta, and the couple lives in Virginia, where they spend most of their life running around after their four children.